The graphic design
idea book

T0103194

Inspiration from 50 masters

Published in Great Britain by
Laurence King Student & Professional
An imprint of Quercus Editions Ltd
Carmelite House
50 Victoria Embankment
London EC4Y 0DZ

An Hachette UK company

Reprinted in 2022

A CIP catalogue record for this book is available
from the British Library

TPB ISBN 978-1-78067-756-9

10 9 8

Design concept: Here Design
Picture research: Peter Kent
Senior Editor: Felicity Maunder

Printed and bound in China by Great Wall Printing

Papers used by Quercus are from well-managed forests
and other responsible sources.

The graphic design
idea book

Inspiration from 50 masters

Josef Albers / Armin Hofmann / David Drummond / Siegfried Odermatt / Michael Bierut / Jan Tschichold / Xanti Schawinsky / Georgii and Vladimir Stenberg / Herbert Matter / Anton Stankowski / Neville Brody / Jessica Hische / Louise Fili / El Lissitzky / Jonathan Barnbrook / Sawdust / Ladislav Sutnar / Paula Scher / Herb Lubalin / Shigeo Fukuda / Alan Fletcher / David Gray / Fons Hickmann / Rolf Müller / Lester Beall / Rex Bonomelli / Paul Rand / Stefan Sagmeister / Fortunato Depero / Saul Bass / Control Group / Karel Teige / Peter Bankov / Seymour Chwast / Marian Bantjes / Bertram Grosvenor Goodhue / Shepard Fairey / Copper Greene / Tibor Kalman / Art Chantry / AG Fronzoni / Gerd Arntz / Otl Aicher / Abram Games / Steff Geissbuhler / Paul Sahre / Massin / Michael Schwab / John Heartfield / Christoph Niemann

Steven Heller and Gail Anderson

Laurence King Publishing

Contents

INTRODUCTION
Make Great Design

There are many ways to make great graphic design. You must have talent; it goes without saying that talent is the ticket to success. But do not forget ambition and desire. So, let's assume you have all these. Then there is the old joke:
'How do you get to Carnegie Hall?' 'Practice, practice, practice!!!'
So now you're ready, right?

No, not exactly!

In addition to these necessary personal strengths, a solid knowledge of visual language, typography, spatial relationships, colour theory, user interaction and many other communication skills are required. This must then all be incorporated into practice and filtered through a keen design instinct and – even more important – imagination. A designer marshals existing tools to creatively communicate messages. A great designer is one whose imagination transcends the existing tools to create opportunities for innovation.

This book does not ensure transcendence or innovation. In fact, the odds are stacked against true innovation, in the sense of creating something never, ever seen before. As Paul Rand enjoyed repeating, 'Being good is hard enough, don't worry about being original.' Yet being good must include a modicum of originality.

What this book does offer is an (admittedly subjective) guide to the various ideas, approaches and themes that designers have used to enhance the quality and effectiveness of their respective works. Graphic design is an amalgam of different components that results in informative, entertaining and commanding visual and textual communications. Our goal is for you to experience the tools (and tropes) that comprise the graphic designer's toolkit, not to copy the examples offered but to be aware that they exist. These techniques and ideas may be viable options or influences for your own work and if they also help you to make really great graphic design, all's the better!

Steven Heller and Gail Anderson

Experiment with design

Josef Albers / Armin Hofmann / David Drummond / Siegfried Odermatt / Michael Bierut / Jan Tschichold / Xanti Schawinsky / Georgii and Vladimir Stenberg / Herbert Matter / Anton Stankowski / Neville Brody

COLOUR
The Magic of Pigment

Josef Albers, one-time Bauhaus master and Yale University professor, was famous for teaching his revolutionary rigid colour theory. He came of age when colour reproduction was difficult and expensive and there were many books and manuals on how to effectively deploy colour in printing and design. Albers' own book, *Interaction of Colour* (1963), rejected mundane approaches to colour, setting down rules for its advantageous use, involving interdisciplinary excursions into science, psychology, aesthetics and magic.

Albers advanced the idea that colour is continually deceptive, and that the exact same colour can evoke innumerable responses depending on how it is seen against other colours. He argued against 'mechanically applying or merely implying laws and rules of colour harmony', because of the subjective nature of perception – it is almost impossible to see a colour by itself and not interacting with its surroundings.

In his famous series *Homage to the Square* (1949–76), Albers explored through hundreds of paintings and prints the optical sensations created by juxtaposing harmonious and disparate colours side by side, in various arrangements and sizes. We can see in this work from the series that the colours interact in sometimes surprising ways. The inner first square is a darker orange yet appears to be less intense than the lighter second square that surrounds it, while the lighter orange of the third square dominates all the shades. Colour hue and intensity are perceptually different depending on the relationship of one square to another.

Since full-colour reproduction is routine today it makes it harder to attain standout results – to achieve impact demands more than simply choosing Pantone numbers. Colour is the designer's ally *and* enemy. So it is wise to look at Albers' practical exercises to understand that colour has a power that designers must tame while appreciating its wild nature.

⊠ Josef Albers, 1967
Homage to the Square –
Within a Thin Interval

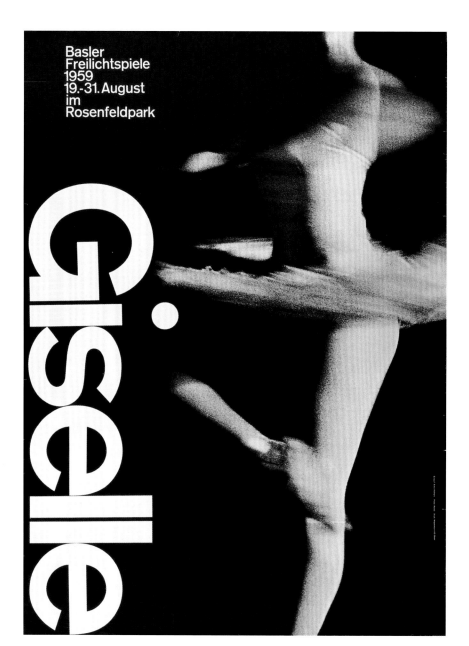

BLACK AND WHITE
Make Monotone Colourful

In the early twentieth century, black and white was common and colour was rare. Now it is the other way around; with current reproduction technologies, black-and-white design is an anomaly. So, why not use the 'millions of colours' that are so freely available on a computer? Maybe because full colour should not be the default solution to all design problems. Given that colour is the norm (though still difficult to use well), designers should challenge themselves to avoid the crutch of colour. Or better yet, to make black-and-white designs more colourful.

Armin Hofmann's poster for this performance of *Giselle* not only looks as fresh as when it was originally designed and printed in 1959, but it shows off the power of black-and-white composition. Hofmann was a leading exponent of the Swiss Style (International Typographic Style) of Modernism, an attempt to reduce design to fundamental type and image based on grids and limited colour palette and typefaces. The Swiss approach was intended to communicate timelessness, and is as relevant today as when it was introduced in the 1950s.

In this poster, the blur of the turning dancer is a counterpoint to the column of sculptural type. The upper- and lower-case Helvetica typeface of Giselle is also rhythmic – the lower-case letters lead the viewer into the action and allow the ballerina a range of motion. Had Hofmann selected all capitals, the letters would have acted as a wall and the kinetic impact of the design would have been diminished.

This poster might have looked fine in colour, but black and white enhances the ballerina's movement and forces the viewer to perceive just the relevant information – title, subject and event – leaving nothing extraneous to distract the eye.

⊠ Armin Hofmann, 1959
Giselle poster

SPOT COLOUR
A Splash of Hue to Focus the Eye

In offset printing, 'spot colour' is used when a designer specifies a unique hue – not made up of CMYK – in order to obtain a more vibrant result. Invariably spot colour is solid and intense, an unfettered swatch of pure pigment. Using it cleverly can produce a dramatic impact, but a subtle application can be just as startling, appearing restrained while in fact drawing the eye immediately where the designer intends. It's not as easy as it sounds – using a spot of colour successfully is dependent on both the colour itself and how and where it is applied, so these choices must be made carefully for deliberate impact.

The Manly Modern is a book about masculinity in post-Second World War Canada. Canadian designer David Drummond found the rationale for his design in the word 'postwar' in the subtitle, which triggered the idea that 'the closest most modern Canadian males come to combat or blood is in the morning shaving ritual'. He has used a black-and-white photograph of a man's face with the only colour being the blood on the piece of tissue, which he says was almost like a badge of courage. Can you see how quickly the eye is drawn to that small swatch?

Understated typography serves to draw even more attention to the small drop of blood seeping through the tissue, the spot of colour that represents a theme of the book. In this case, anything other than a black-and-white photo would not have delivered the same contrast and would have been far less effective. One of the designer's most challenging decisions is what *not* to include so that the power of the spot colour is not overshadowed by extraneous effects.

The Manly Modern

Masculinity in Postwar Canada

CHRISTOPHER DUMMITT

⊠ David Drummond, 1999
The Manly Modern
book cover

⊠ Siegfried Odermatt, 1960
Advertisement
for Neuenburger
Versicherungen

FLAT COLOUR
Switching off the Gloss

One-colour and four-colour printing approaches are at either end of the printing spectrum. In fact, four-colour is so economical these days that one-colour printing is used as an anomaly, to grab attention. But let's not forget two-colour printing, and more specifically one-colour plus black. This can be a mighty fine and aesthetically startling combination. The addition of one flat or matt colour can offer excellent opportunities for contrast, especially light against dark hues.

There are countless ways to use this method and one of the most impressive examples is in a 1960 series of cautionary advertisements by Swiss designer Siegfried Odermatt for the Neuenburger Versicherungen insurance company.

At play in each advertisement is a fragmented black-and-white photograph seen in concert with a single-word headline, which is printed in a bright, contrasting colour. Here, a car smashes into the word 'Car'; elsewhere in the series an X-ray of a broken bone lies on top of the broken word 'Accident', or shards of broken windshield cut through the word 'Glass'. In each case almost two-thirds of the image area is left empty, forcing the eye down to the meat of the message.

Flat colour is not just a supporting actor in this poster, it makes or breaks the viewer's perception. Had this headline been printed in black or grey it might still be eye-catching, but applying the additional colour illuminates the entire concept. Odermatt's choice of flat colour is both strategic and aesthetic, and creates a tone that has strength without being aggressive. Giving colour such a key role is a useful tool and fun technique to use.

OVERLAPPING COLOURS
One plus One Equals Many

For decades designers have been using overlapping colours as a visual effect, exploring the multitude of colour possibilities opened up by mixing CMYK. Perhaps there is something comforting – or even magical – about watching these colours combine to make new hues and liquid-like patterns. Overlapping colour was a common trope in mid-century Modernist graphic design that represented contemporaneity. Arguably, this was the rebirth of colour, following the grey austerity of the war and immediate post-war years.

Michael Bierut's 2013 logo for the fine paper manufacturer Mohawk is an M that cleverly suggests rolls of paper in motion, highlighted by the Modernist motif of overlapping transparent colour. Bierut explains his approach as freeing him from the past restrictions of a vintage trademark showing the profile of a native American, which had limited the Mohawk logo to almost always being printed in understated monochrome. The new logo is perfect for both print and screen, as it allows the colourful graphics to be as vibrant and varied as needed. Colour – which changes with each application of the logo – is Bierut's tool for making the logo look different yet recognizable every time it is used.

This ability to create numerous colourways further enables designers to play with this most versatile of toolkit devices. Colour impacts mood, attitude and meaning; overlapping colour only increases this potential. As Bierut said of his design, 'the hardest part was reducing all the different colours and combinations that looked fantastic to a practical number'.

⊠ Michael Bierut, 2013
Mohawk Fine Papers logo

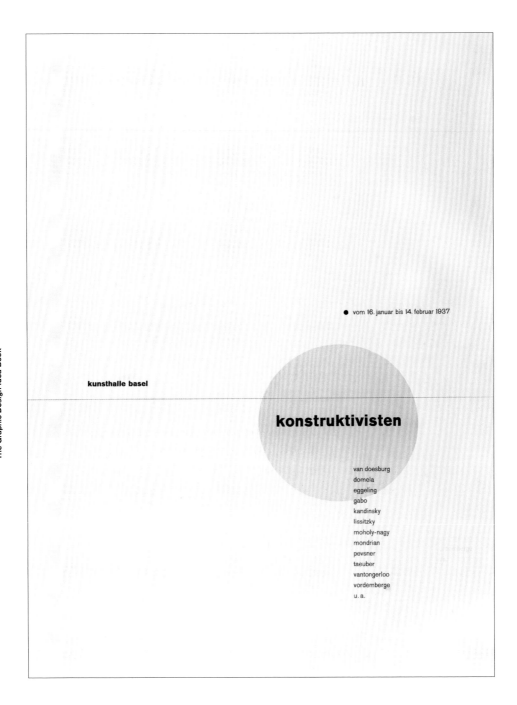

⊠ Jan Tschichold, 1937
Konstruktivisten
exhibition poster

WHITE SPACE
Liberating the Printed Page

'It's not what you put in, it's what you leave out', in relation to the use of white space, is as true for graphic design as it is for painting and drawing. During the nineteenth century, magazine and newspaper compositors filled up every inch of available space with text and, sometimes, image. The concept of empty or negative space was anathema to publishers, who refused to waste even a pica of editorial real estate on nothingness. It was only when it became difficult to distinguish the advertisements from the editorial that white space was added, as a frame. Around the late 1920s the floodgates opened when white space became a valuable asset.

Jan Tschichold's poster for the 1937 Constructivist exhibition at the Kunsthalle, Basel, is an elegantly functional example of the use of white space. It was a breath of fresh air in the graphic design world of the time, all the more so as it followed on from the German tradition of graphic design, where blackletter was tightly squeezed into massive, airless text blocks. Tschichold's poster represents the full force of what he called 'asymmetric typography', as well as showing how emptiness can make even minimal type more striking.

Tschichold lines up the type – title, participants, date and venue – on his tight grid, the invisible frame that defines the layout, careful to leave precise amounts of space between the typographic elements. A thin line, which serves as a horizon, carves the spotlight of colour illuminating the word '*konstruktivisten*', which is exactly where the eye is meant to land, and divides the page itself – the eye uses that line as a plane to divide the information. The poster is liberated of extraneous material, leaving the message as pristine as possible. Although the layout is subdued it is made memorable through its elegant simplicity.

GEOMETRY
Shapes as Symbols

The geometric hieroglyphs that emerged in graphic design of the 1930s and 1940s are a common Modernist trope that is still in use today. At the time, conventional realist illustrations were considered passé and stylized art deco visuals too fussy, so the universal graphic shapes – triangles, squares, circles (the Bauhaus trinity), broken lines and lozenges – were used to signal a subtle contemporary approach that was not tied to the moorings of earlier styles and fashions, and represented newness.

This 1934 poster for Olivetti, designed by former Bauhaus teacher Xanti Schawinsky, although based strictly on a grid, achieves a layout that appears fluid. The randomly placed Olivetti lozenge echoes the unusual curvilinear cropping of the typewriter keys. Against the field of beige, intersecting random lines are anchors that hold down the floating graphic elements, resulting in a futuristic sensibility. If not for the old typewriter keys it would be difficult to assign a date to this poster. Even the name Olivetti is set in a typewriter face that is as crisp and clean as a digital output.

Even today, the use of geometry by designers is symbolic of a unique moment when graphic design was freed from the rigours of central axis composition (type that was centred on the page and justified left and right). Paul Rand once said there is nothing more pure than geometry, so setting type in and around geometric forms is as classic and functional for today's utilitarian design as it ever was. There is nothing more eye-catching than the circle, square and triangle in any configuration, perhaps adding in a broken line or lozenge for a little extra geometrical spice.

⊠ Xanti Schawinsky, 1934
Olivetti poster

PERSPECTIVE
Creating Visual Points of View

Graphic design is essentially flat and one-dimensional, unless it happens to contain an illustration that shows depth and height. So to achieve certain pictorial effects and points of view it is necessary to apply perspective.

This 1929 film poster by Russian avant-garde designers Georgii and Vladimir Stenberg, created for Dziga Vertov's *Man with a Movie Camera*, is dynamic because of its perspective. The poster is rendered in two dimensions but gives the illusion of three. Those huge skyscrapers thrusting skyward to some infinite end point force the eye to rise up and towards the falling figure. The sense of height and the frozen yet impending fall is so intense that it feels vertiginous and, together with the disembodied figure, suggests a psychologically nightmarish perspective. The poster's bottom-up viewpoint also echoes Vertov's famously disorienting cinematic camera angles.

It is unlikely that film posters today could be as artfully enigmatic as this one, which lacks the hard sell of contemporary specimens. Yet the Stenberg brothers' means of baiting and catching the eye through radical perspectives and a jarring colour palette is appropriate for any design era. This poster may not overtly tell the plot of the film or showcase its stars but its perspective hypnotically pulls the viewer into the vortex of the image with the aim of selling a movie ticket.

⊠ Georgii and Vladimir Stenberg, 1929
Man with a Movie Camera film poster

Experiment with Design

SCALE
The Value of Extremes

Most people love miniature things like poodles, horses and cars. But graphic designers often prefer large over small. Paula Scher's 2002 monograph titled *Make It Bigger* refers to the widely held myth that anything made bigger is better design, which she shows is a fallacy. Yet contrast between large and small scale can be very striking.

In this 1935 Swiss tourism poster designed by Herbert Matter, it is the juxtaposition of the exaggerated, heroic blown-up figure in the foreground and the smaller skier swooping down the slopes in the background that gives the piece its majesty and memorability. Matter was a master of photography and montage, and the deliberate scale relationship between the principal and secondary figures – a recurrent technique in his Swiss Tourist Board promotions of the 1930s – takes this poster out of the realm of the commonplace travel ad. It is virtually impossible not to be engaged by this composition, which perhaps explains why it is among the masterpieces of twentieth-century poster art.

Matter's success with this piece is largely down to the fact that the proportional shift in scale has the effect of making a two-dimensional space seem like a three-dimensional one, which in turn draws the viewer into the image as a participant in this virtual environment. He forces the eye to embrace the players on this stage, so that the viewer can identify with either the main figure or the secondary skier. Two other elements are key to the composition's success: the cool crispness that dominates the colour palette evokes the cold of winter on the slopes, while the radical shift in scale also emphasizes the mountain on which the figures are skiing. All these factors combine to admirably articulate the message of the poster.

☒ Herbert Matter, 1935
Pontresina poster

Experiment with Design

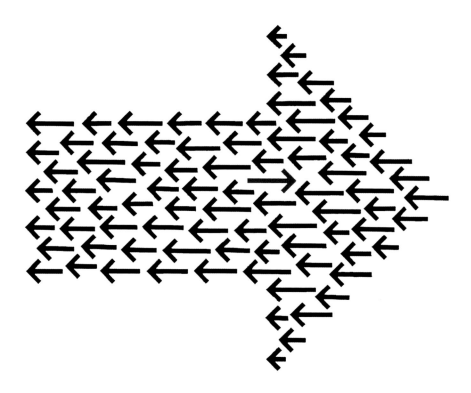

CONCEPTUAL DESIGN
When an Idea Drives Form

———————— **What we'll call conceptual design is where the visual idea influences the physical form it takes. In other words, the concept governs the look of the design. Designers working in the realm of ideas have a tendency to either overthink or underthink a concept, when they should strike a balance between form and content. Conceptual design demands discipline to marshal the individual design elements – type, image, lettering – in the communication of a harmonious outcome. One element alone cannot fulfil the goal; everything must work together as a whole.**

A very simple illustration of successful conceptual design is German designer Anton Stankowski's 1972 depiction of a forward-thrusting arrow made from retreating arrows. At first glance the form seems to be constructed like a school of fish following a leader – in this case arrow glyphs. In fact the glyphs are in a backward charge, with a hero of sorts, a red arrow, surrounded by the conformist black arrows, defiantly moving forward and leading the charge against conformity.

Stankowski often used arrows to represent larger human concepts instead of resorting to sentimental or emotional realism. And it works. The arrow is a highly charged symbol that dictates behaviour, so to apply it in such a way gives it instant recognition, even if it invites multiple interpretations. Stare long enough and it is simply a pattern. Read it as an illustration and meanings pour out: it could be seen as running away, or, since red is a charged colour, as heading towards something exciting, or ominous.

Message-driven design can be difficult to pull off but when the concept and form are seamless, the audience is given a cognitive gift designed to aid comprehension.

⊠ Anton Stankowski, 1972
From *Der Pfeil: Spiel, Gleichnis, Kommunikation*
(*The Arrow: Game, Allegory, Communication*)

IMPROVISATION
Riff on Icons

Great design involves large doses of improvisational energy both before and after deciding on a specific visual direction. Only the most rigid systems are ever really locked in stone. Good design is, after all, about exercising creative licence. The power to play and discover is central to design practice of all kinds, and improvisation is key to what Paul Rand heralded as 'the play-principle'.

Arguably, all creative endeavours involve some level of improvisation to get to the refinement stage. For a designer, moving elements around just to make sparks fly – and not entirely knowing what the end result will be – is essential to surprise, and surprise is more often than not the very reaction designers want from their audience. Design improvisation can begin as a loose sketching process, helping to discard all constraints, or, as is common in jazz, it can riff on a very specific theme.

Taking as a starting point its most recognizable brand asset – the bottle – Coca-Cola asked 36 designers to reimagine the brand and create different iterations and incarnations, both decorative and conceptual. The bottle and its signature colours act as anchors for the brand (although a few of the invited designers were limited to black and white), while any imaginative tangent was possible. Neville Brody's response to the brief was to retain the bottle itself as the focal point while exaggerating the so-called Coke 'wave' in a hypnotically optical fashion. Retaining a recognizable element is an anchor for the viewer that gave Brody licence to play with colour and pattern.

If you attempt to improvise in this way, just watch as the hand automatically draws your unbridled thoughts on paper or screen. What starts as simple doodles quickly evolves into more realized notions. Riffing on well-known iconic forms provides touchstones that prevent designs from straying too far, but any kind of improvisational activity keeps the hand, eye and mind limber and poised to solve design problems.

⊠ Neville Brody, 2014
Poster for Coca-Cola's
Coke Bottle 100 project

Play with type and image

Jessica Hische / Louise Fili / El Lissitzky / Jonathan Barnbrook / Sawdust / Ladislav Sutnar / Paula Scher / Herb Lubalin / Shigeo Fukuda / Alan Fletcher / David Gray

SIGNATURE LETTER
Big, Bold and Symbolic

With a signature letter you can almost sit back and allow your assignment to design itself. Well, *almost* but not quite. The signature letter is like the cornerstone of a building or the personality of a specific layout or composition. From the letter grows everything else.

What is meant by a signature letter is usually a large, capital letter, sometimes machine-set, other times hand-drawn, with a decorative filigree or symbolic ornament as part of its structural design. It can be almost any letter, but O is the purest geometrically and X is most impactful symbolically. As the first and last letters in the alphabet, A and Z have great power, and by virtue of being extra wide, M and W are startling. Whatever the letter, it must always be visually and contextually more important than anything else on a page. In this way it is the signature letter.

A striking initial capital at the beginning of a paragraph sets the visual and narrative tone of a story. Interestingly, the examples here, designed by Jessica Hische, are not 'start caps' but front-cover illustrations – logo-like introductions to a series of venerable classics published by Penguin Books. From Jane Austen's *Pride and Prejudice* via James Joyce's *A Portrait of the Artist as a Young Man* to Carlos Ruiz Zafón's *The Shadow of the Wind*, each is the first letter of the author's last name, a veritable signet, embellished in a way that represents either the author's life or the time and place of the plot. These are alphabetic illustrations that unify the entire A to Z series, while standing alone on their aesthetic virtues.

Quirkiness is not the only qualification for a signature letter – there are many kinds of monumental letter with and without decorative excesses – but it must be large enough and bold enough to hold the space and draw attention to itself, acting much like a beckoning beacon or sign.

JANE AUSTEN

PRIDE AND PREJUDICE

Jessica Hische, 2011
Penguin Drop Caps
book covers

SCULPTING TYPE
Text Becomes Illustration

In graphic design, 'form' refers to the visual configuration of an object, its structure and the relationship between its parts and its style. Graphic designers are adept at taking key parts of one visual idea to make another, which, without demeaning designers, is arguably the typographic equivalent of someone creating an animal out of balloons – yet more functional, of course.

There are, however, limitations to what one can accomplish with modelling balloons, but the sky's the limit for how type and image can be cast or contorted into shapes that express a concept. This is famously represented by New York designer Louise Fili's sculpted copyright pages, which have become a staple of the dozens of books she has created over a long career, and through which an otherwise mundane element of book design is made more vibrant. These pages are set pieces that serve as a typographic signature.

Copyright information, mandatory and essential, is routinely typeset more or less as an afterthought. But Fili's designs, in which typeset copy is configured into the shape of an object related to the book's contents, are worth savouring – and perhaps even reading. The copyright information for a book about the best tea places in England forms the shape of a steaming cup of tea, while that for a book called *You Can't Be Too Careful: Cautionary Tales for the Impetuous, Curious, and Blithely Oblivious* is designed in the shape of a gravestone, a witty comment on the book itself.

Using content to create form and structure is not limited to copyright pages. It is one of the ways in which designers can achieve a witty departure from conventional typesetting and give the user more of a reason to read something that might ordinarily be ignored.

⊠ Louise Fili, 1992
Copyright page for *You Can't Be Too Careful*

LETTERING AS IMAGE
Illustrating with Letterforms

Creating images from letterforms and making letters into pictures is an essential graphic design skill that goes in and out of fashion over the decades. Around the turn of the twentieth century, illustrative lettering – contorting people or things into letterforms – was a common means of telling a story in western European illumination. After repeated use it became clichéd, but around the early 1920s the practice was modernized by figures including the Russian Constructivist designer El Lissitzky.

His 1928 poster *Four (Arithmetic) Actions* was created in the Russian Constructivist style of composing (or constructing) metal typecase material to form characters and pictures. Lissitzky employs letters of the Cyrillic alphabet as the bodies of a crew of symbolic beings that each have a role in the story. The CCCP (the Russian name for the USSR, or Union of Soviet Socialist Republics) have legs and heads and are holding banners, while other letters are marching triumphantly over a hammer and sickle. Like stick figures on steroids, this approach to design was at once a witty departure from serious propaganda and a novel way to feed a message to the masses. Anything this playful – indeed cartoony – has to have positive connotations. Like trade characters, these guys are friends not foes.

When using this method, however, designers tread a fine line between the cleverly appropriate and the stupidly kitsch. How and into what form the letters are transformed can mean the difference between effective and superficial communication. Lissitzky's poster succeeded because it was created in the form of a comic strip or children's picture story. The signs, symbols and letters of the composition combine to tell a tale of the evolving Soviet Union. Lissitzky's piece has become recognized as a period style and should be a touchstone for contemporary practice, not a template to copy.

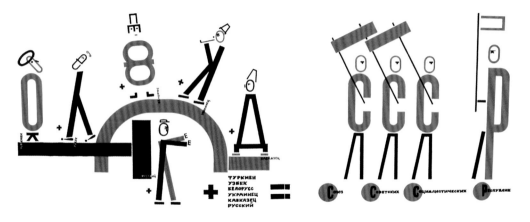

⊠ El Lissitzky, 1928
Four (Arithmetic) Actions

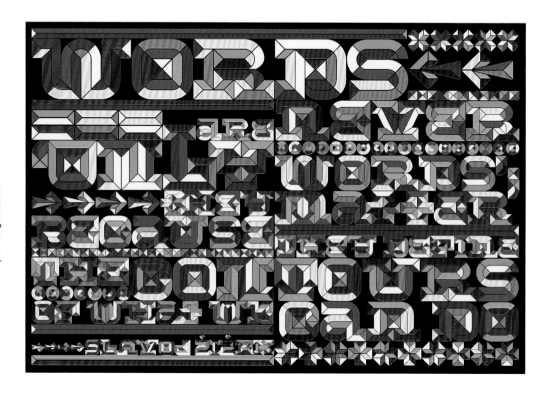

 Jonathan Barnbrook and
Jonathan Abbott, 2011
*Words Are Never Only
Words*

ILLEGIBILITY
Readability Be Damned

If legibility is a definition of good typography, then it follows that illegibility is a sign of bad typography. Yet this does not account for readability, where something readable does not always have to be conventionally legible – it can evoke an idea in a pictorial language. Whether type is deemed readable or unreadable depends entirely on the context in which it is conceived and also the context in which it is read. Some of the most readable typography will be illegible for those who do not have the patience to read it. Decipherability is rooted in fluency with certain familiar codes, so something may be conventionally unreadable but still perfectly cogent with the right key – think of the Rosetta Stone.

Jonathan Barnbrook and Jonathan Abbott's typographic composition commemorating the revolutions of the 2011 Arab Spring was designed itself to be revolutionary. Revolutions, they reasoned, are driven through action but are spread through ideas and language. In this typographic melange the aim was to show the power of language to emerge from the chaos; in the words of cultural theorist Slavoj Žižek, reproduced on the piece: 'Words are never "only words". They matter because they define the contours of what we can do.'

Here the sanctity of individual letters and words is rejected in favour of connecting all the words together, making each letter a part of a pattern that is perceived as both word and image. From a distance the lettering is about patterns, but up close words materialize. This piece is about revealing hidden or coded messages. It requires work on the reader's part, but the act of deciphering makes the message even more valuable to the receiver – and probably more memorable. The styles may vary but the technique of hide and seek can be applied to any design on every theme.

NUMBERS
When the Figures Add Up

Numbers are as integral to graphic design as letters, and can be just as expressive. Whether used as page numbers or in a demonstrative role as, say, a chapter opener of a book, the price on a supermarket sign or even the numbers on a clock, it's worth remembering that the more deliberate the design of the numeral, the more effective the impact of the message. Arabic numerals are commonly used with most languages – and are often the only recognizable typographic characters in many non-Latin scripts. Roman numerals are also used, though less frequently and without much variation from the original.

There are a few ways to consider designing with numbers – let's count them. The first is as part of a type family and how the individual figures fit together with upper- and lower-case letters. The second is creating numbers that express a visual idea, where the numeral is used for its symbolic associations (such as a 1 to represent a skyscraper). The third is stylization of numerals to create an illustrative or otherwise eccentric number set. Then there is the approach that borrows from all three categories to create numerals that stand alone on their own graphic weight, endowed with visual strength or symbolic meaning, like these by London's Sawdust studio.

The numbers 1 to 9, made of straight, curvilinear and concentric black lines, are visually hypnotic, skilfully crafted to simulate ribbon. The handsome linear motif and the ribbon's subtle three-dimensionality result in a soothing, eye-catching style. While all the numbers have charm, arguably the 4 is the most charming of all because it looks exactly like a ribbon that serendipitously became a number. As this set was custom-designed for a client (as an interpretation of medals awarded for excellence), it may have limited direct applications. But conceptually, making typographic design based on familiar elements is a model for other designs.

⊠ Sawdust, 2013
Numbers designed for the Shanghai Jiao Tong Top 200 Research Universities Encyclopedia

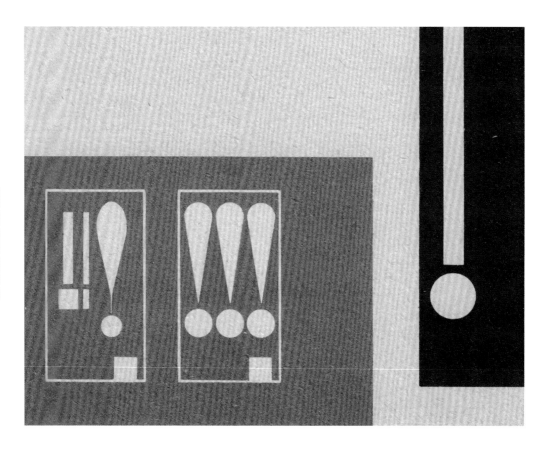

PUNCTUATION MARKS
The Rise of Functional Decoration

Punctuation marks are used in graphic design to enhance – indeed add rhythm to – written and visual language by adding emphasis, indicating questions and creating dramatic pauses. They are traffic signs that tell the reader where and when to slow down, stop, go or wait. When graphically employed, the simplest typographic punctuation can be used to suggest broader linguistic concepts – minus the words.

Czech-born designer Ladislav Sutnar made use of punctuation as both a graphic and linguistic device, enlarging, repeating and otherwise transforming it into functional decoration. Starting in the late 1940s his punctuation methods, however, were employed to help the reader navigate pages of unillustrated text in books and brochures. In the 1950s he also began using punctuation marks as icons in his design. Believing that the public was familiar with exclamation points and question marks, they could serve a dual purpose by suggesting an idea while adding a weighty graphic element to a page.

Designers today use punctuation marks in both conceptual and decorative ways; while Sutnar was not averse to some decoration, he insisted that every element on the page had a rational purpose in editorial and advertising contexts. Through his work with punctuation he influenced what in the 1990s became a more widespread use of typographical icons that are now essential to digital platforms like apps.

⊠ Ladislav Sutnar, 1958
Advertisement for
Vera Scarves

TRANSFORMATION
Turning One Thing into Another

Transformation – animating design elements from one form into another – is one of the many joys of designing with digital tools. Allowing for objects to kinetically change or morph helps transform ideas from ethereal notions into concrete visuals; paper and screen are transformed from empty vessels into works full of meaning, and audiences are transformed from passive to active participants.

Designers use all, or some, of the methods and devices touched on in this book to achieve these transformations, but the most likely way to capture and influence a viewer is through the transformative power of surprise. Achieving surprise is never easy, as design requires planning, organizing and categorizing, which invariably removes serendipity from the process. Animation helps the designer to inject the unexpected; it is the tool that is currently bringing on much change in graphic design.

The key to transformation is to reject that which is literal or expected. How is this done? It starts with understanding how a design problem can be looked at it in a different way to achieve an alternative result. If a client asks for a logo, maybe your answer is to design several which describe the institution's different facets. Perhaps, rather than thinking of that logo as static, you could reimagine it as something fluid or kinetic.

Paula Scher's identity for the Philadelphia Museum of Art describes an institution that has many assets in its collection. The logo itself is built around the word 'Art', which transforms every time it is used. The dynamic change from one A to another enables the museum to show as many different identities as it has works of art. This randomization ensures the logo is always transforming and always surprising (within the limits of the specific images that are selected) and the logo can be modified for exhibitions and collections. The logo is alive. The brand is memorable. The museum is given a new identity and the public is given a visual plaything.

⊠ Paula Scher, 2014
Philadelphia Museum
of Art logo identity

VISUAL PUNS
Two or More Meanings at Once

All designers are inherently visual punsters. A visual pun is an image with two or more meanings that, when combined, yield a single, concise, yet often layered or even coded message. Like a child's rebus, the confluence of signs, symbols, pictures and letters take the viewer on a cognitive journey into realms of representation and interpretation. Deciphering a pun offers a mnemonic payoff – and it is hard to ignore or forget something that takes any time to understand. Visual puns are also witty in profound, sardonic and slapstick ways, which provide intellectual and visceral satisfaction to the viewer.

Verbal puns are often painfully, wonderfully ham-fisted, while visual puns cannot succeed without nuance and subtlety. Typographic puns involve combining two or more types of pictorial elements to create a sign or symbol that encapsulates a witty new idea. Herb Lubalin and Tom Carnase's iconic 1965 *Mother and Child* magazine logo is a classic example of this. An ampersand sits inside the 'o' of 'Mother', suggesting a baby in the womb. It does not take long to decipher the composition that reads simultaneously as word and picture. It is functional and symbolic – a double whammy that continues to bring visual revelation decades after it was created.

Visual puns like this are conceptually economical. The idea is conveyed and a mood is established through a minimum of graphic effort – which is the essence of an unforgettable pun.

⊠ Herb Lubalin and
Tom Carnase, 1965
Mother and Child
magazine logo

ILLUSION
Arrest and Intrigue

Illusion is the magician's stock-in-trade. It is also a designer's mainstay, but difficult to accomplish successfully without obscuring a message. In graphic design, a thing is almost never seen as it really is, to paraphrase Josef Albers. The role of optical puzzles in design is to reveal a curious clarity and provide memorability.

Shigeo Fukuda, Japan's master of graphic illusionism, made his literal and figurative mark by tweaking the mind's eye. Believing that actively solving puzzles was more enjoyable and memorable than passively being handed a message on a tray, he routinely challenged his viewers to interpret the meaning of his political, social and commercial work.

Fukuda designed this poster to promote a 1975 exhibition of his graphics at the Keio Department Store in Tokyo. At first glance the pattern is more abstract than representational, but that's just a tease. The high-contrast imagery convinces the eye that nothing and something is happening at the same time. The work could illustrate tension in the proverbial battle between the sexes through the piano-key alternating pattern of a high-kicking male leg in black, punctuated by the female leg formed by the white space. Yet it could mean a lot of things.

While Fukuda never entirely shares his true message, mystery, in concert with his graphic skill, is his ally in drawing people to his exhibition, where they may or may not find the answer. Using graphically arresting illusion to subtly vex yet enlighten the viewer is part of a game plan that absorbs an audience in your work for longer than a split second.

⊠ Shigeo Fukuda, 1975
Keio Department Store
exhibition poster

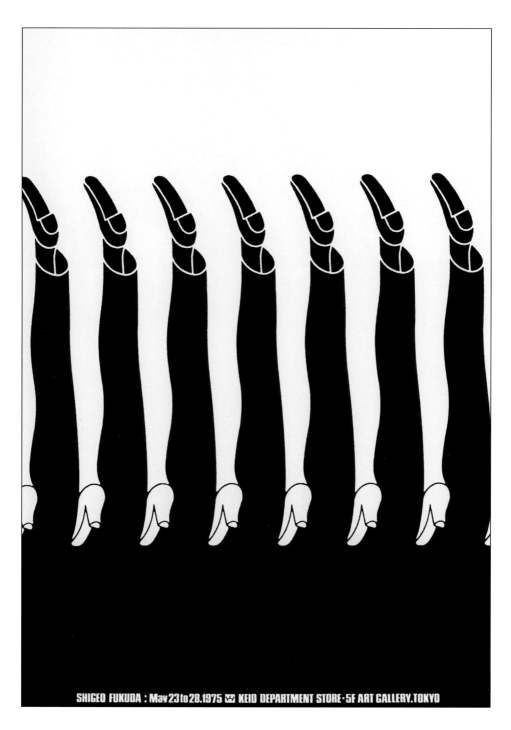

SHIGEO FUKUDA : May 23 to 28.1975 ☒ KEIO DEPARTMENT STORE·5F ART GALLERY.TOKYO

TROMPE L'OEIL
Fooling the Eye

Art in two dimensions is not as dynamic as in three. As far back as ancient Greece and Rome, artists have developed deceptively simple ways of achieving three-dimensional illusions, such as faux windows or doors on two-dimensional surfaces, or blank walls to fool the eye by introducing perspective that did not exist. During the Baroque period, the age of decorative excess, what became known as *trompe l'oeil* (or fooling the eye) was a form of perceptual hijinks. For comic relief artists even painted exact replicas of house flies on otherwise serious paintings.

Graphic designers found the technique was improved somewhat by the invention of the airbrush in 1876. Used for photo retouching and highlights, commercial artists found they could make more realistic pictorial illusions to fool the average viewer, which captured attention for the product or idea that was being illustrated.

Using pictorial illusion on a grand scale is guaranteed to attract a double take and be memorable. This was the goal of London designer Alan Fletcher's 1962 bus siding advertisement, which shows the bottom halves of six bus passengers sitting on the letters of the words 'Pirelli Slippers', lined up with the real windows of a London double-decker bus. From the street it looks like the people on the bus are actually sitting on the letters. It is an interactive illusion that both startles and fools – and is impossible to ignore.

Fletcher earned success by being the first to use the bus siding so smartly and imposingly. After it was launched, the audacious concept began to earn infectious audience popularity (much like viral advertising today), with bus riders actively wanting to sit at seats at the windows over the sign. If Instagram had been around in 1962, this campaign would have generated a slew of pictures! *Trompe l'oeil* continues to garner delight from unsuspecting viewers with its infinite potential for cleverness.

⊠ Alan Fletcher, 1962
Pirelli Slippers bus
advertisement

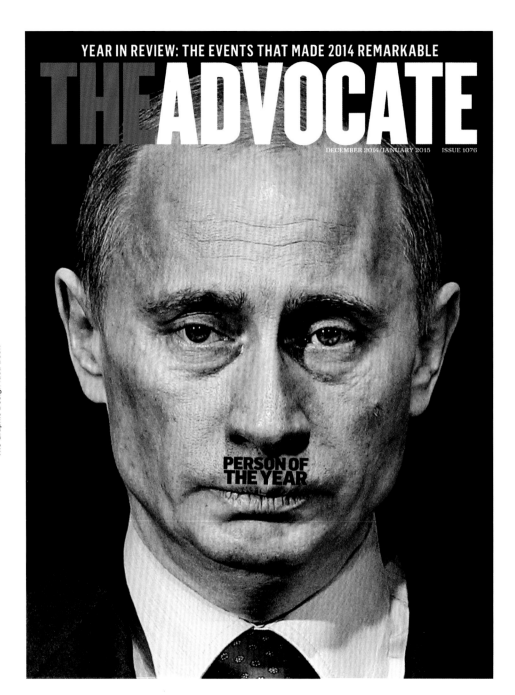

YEAR IN REVIEW: THE EVENTS THAT MADE 2014 REMARKABLE

THE ADVOCATE

DECEMBER 2014/JANUARY 2015   ISSUE 1076

PERSON OF THE YEAR

☒ David Gray, 2014
The Advocate
magazine cover

IRONY

When Something Is
Not What It Seems

**Saying one thing but meaning another, in order to be funny
or to make a point, is the essence of irony. Irony in graphic design is a
combination of text and picture that has a double meaning. One of the
designer's most effective tools for making irony is the visual pun, and,
just as humour makes messages memorable, irony gives indelibility
to understanding.**

Brooklyn-based designer David Gray's 2014 cover for
The Advocate magazine is needle-sharp irony – a biting attack on the
threatening stance Russian president Vladimir Putin is taking on the world
stage and at home. Building on the West's perception of Putin as a dictator,
Gray references the twentieth century's most heinous leader by positioning
the headline 'Person of the Year' in a panel that mimics Adolf Hitler's
moustache over Putin's upper lip.

Gray does not directly accuse Putin of being another Hitler;
instead, the composition allows the reader to decide. But the implication
is as clear as the nose on Putin's face. That cold look of this former KGB
agent who became Russian Prime Minister comes with its own inherent
identifiers, but these are heightened and underlined by the positioning of
that headline, set in two lines of bold, sans-serif capital type. The overall
result is suggestive of a Big Brother poster. A vivid typographic point is
made, but more importantly irony reigns and the viewer is not only informed
but entertained.

Explore media and techniques

Fons Hickmann / Rolf Müller / Lester Beall / Rex Bonomelli / Paul Rand / Stefan Sagmeister / Fortunato Depero / Saul Bass / Control Group

BLUR
Drama in Two Dimensions

To blur something and give it a spectral look is to hide its true form from view, and suggest something mysterious or otherworldly. It is also a means to make a static object or figure – as well as type and lettering – appear to be kinetic in two-dimensional static space. Blurring, which is often rejected as a mistake when it happens in photography, is an important element of modern art and has risen to the level of virtuosity in graphic design.

Blurring works best when it is clearly intentional and there is no question of its being an error. An accidental blur can be useful, but actually applying that accident to the work requires skill.

Berlin designer Fons Hickmann's *The Nonexisting Nothing* exquisitely employs the blur technique for maximum impact. The poster was made for an exhibition entitled *Man and God* and its starting point was the Shroud of Turin – the ancient cloth said to bear the outline of Christ's facial features. The shroud's authenticity is the subject of scholarly debate, and here the blurred spectre bathed in luminescent yellow expresses both the mystery behind the claim, and the title of the exhibition.

If the poster image were a literal portrait, the visual perception and intellectual impact would be lessened. Blurring the image makes it enigmatic and encourages the viewer to engage emotionally as well as perceptually with the picture and message. Rather than distorting, blur can provide the clarity that a perfectly focused poster might not.

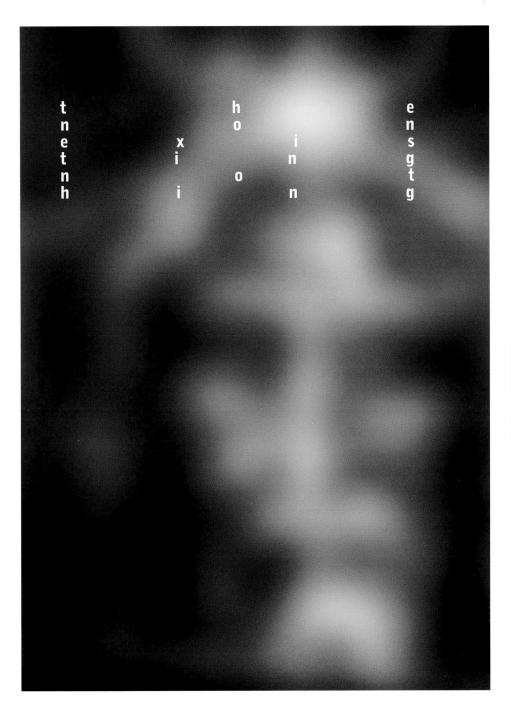

⊠ Fons Hickmann, 2007
The Nonexisting Nothing

⊠ Rolf Müller, 1972
Kieler Woche poster

DISTORTION
Manipulation Alters Perception

Before the computer made possible a wide range of easy-to-achieve distortion effects, designers manipulated type and image using various time-consuming manual techniques. The French book designer Massin contorted all the dialogue text in his 1964 graphic interpretation of *The Bald Soprano* by printing it on rubber sheets then stretching them in the desired direction to be photographed. With the advent in the 1960s of the PhotoTypositor (a photographic headline typesetting machine), radical condensing, elongating and expanding of type using anamorphic lenses was made possible. Typographic distortion is one of many tools a designer can use to achieve an abstract quality.

There are many examples to illustrate this technique, but Rolf Müller's 1972 *Kieler Woche* poster is the quintessence of simplicity and elegance. Undulating a few typeset words and numbers, suggesting sails blowing in the wind against a sky of blue, the designer announces the dates of this famous annual boating event in northern Germany, which had been publicized by many posters showing boats and sails, both realistic and abstract, over the years. Distortion was a staple of modern art that had been appropriated in commercial art and design, but the abstracted simplification of this poster breathed fresh life into it.

Typographic distortion can alter perceptions and can sometimes throw the viewer off balance. Yet rather than shock the senses, Müller's design revels in its own soothing, satisfied simplicity. But it takes patience: to create the perfect evocation of pulling a sail forward through distortion is not as easy as it looks. Nuance is key and just a pica stretched or condensed the wrong way could ruin the entire concept.

LAYERING
One Image Made from Many

Layering is a defining characteristic of Modernist graphic design that appears in the work of many designers from the 1930s through into the 1950s. It is based on photo collaging and montaging disparate images at varying scales for dramatic impact. The images are often illuminated by colours, both solid and transparent, either washing over a picture or separating one from another. Layering has a timeless quality as its Modernist approach is still effectively used today – and not just as nostalgia.

Lester Beall, a key figure in American Modernist graphic design, was influenced by the Bauhaus in Europe and was especially fascinated with László Moholy-Nagy's photograms. Beall's posters of the 1930s and 1940s are known for their compositions of concept-driven imagery derived from a broad assortment of photographs, illustrations and engravings, which he combined with flat fields of colour and bold typography. His U.S. government promotions for the Rural Electrification Administration use iconic imagery and spare typography to convey notions of social service. This 1948 cover for *Scope*, the house magazine of the Upjohn pharmaceutical company, is typical of his distinctive layering. He used this artistic approach for scientific material because it offered a functional approach while also packing a visual punch.

What makes this composition so startling is the open hand with the bullseye of bacteria in the palm. When creating images of this kind, there must be a focal point like this. By juxtaposing it with the smoking woman in black and white, silhouetted on a tri-colour surface, this potentially lacklustre collection of disparate images is made dynamic. For layering to be successful, all the pieces have to work in a kind of harmonic dissonance in terms of subject and scale.

⊠ Lester Beall, 1948
Scope magazine cover

AGEING
Something Borrowed
and Something New

When a certain subject calls for a 'heritage' look, a contemporary piece of design can be turned into an instant artefact from the past. This is often done for book covers as well as food and drink labels. Vintage things can seem more loved, more historically significant, and more 'real'. Ageing gives the illusion of gravitas, and fools the eye into believing that the work was created by hand. But beware – though a convincingly aged design bestows a sense of nostalgia, a poorly or inappropriately aged piece just looks musty and will send the wrong signal to the audience. The trick is to find a balance. The designer must subtly signal that it is a facsimile of the old that they are looking at, rather than trying to fake oldness.

American designer Rex Bonomelli recreated an old newspaper as the jacket for Stephen King's novel *11/22/63*. The jacket is literally torn across the top to reveal the title printed on the cover, recalling the famous tagline from 1940s film noir advertisements, 'torn from the front pages'. The design successfully mimics the ephemeral quality of a yellowing 1960s newspaper, and enables the designer to fit a lot of key information, including additional type and photographs, on the front without sacrificing aesthetics.

Bonomelli's design is a departure from the slick jackets usually seen on King's books, which are in the prevailing 'bestseller' style, with shiny foil type. But since this novel was King's first book of historical fiction, Bonomelli thought it appropriate to do something different with the cover. The newspaper design is accurate to the era, and even the type for the bestselling author's name is sufficiently battered. The look is serious and important, with the torn paper and deep red background adding a layer of suspense.

Importantly, Bonomelli's distressed type and image conceit is not just a gimmick, rather it sets a tone that moves the narrative forward. Ageing is best used when there is a good reason for it.

⊠ Rex Bonomelli, 2011
11/22/63 book cover

COLLAGE
Create Graphic Design Puzzles

The Graphic Design Idea Book

Cutting and sticking papers together to make pictures is a kindergarten staple. It is also a proven means of experimenting with the formal relationships in art and design, and can be accomplished by virtually anyone, artist or not. Designers know it as an enduring method of creating serendipitous (and oddball) juxtapositions that through compositional alchemy can result in strong graphics.

Modern collage media may be traced to the early 1900s when Pablo Picasso and Juan Gris stuck printed clippings from newspapers and magazines onto their Cubist artworks. Today's graphic designers, rather than using scissors and glue, create collage by following a clipping path on the computer screen and moving the various pieces with a mouse or stylus.

American Modernist graphic designer Paul Rand worked with paper and glue from a stock of torn papers, stock photographs and found pictorial remnants. He wrote that, 'Collage is a very ingenious … method of working because it abbreviates the time it takes to express a meaning by the process of juxtaposition.' While decidedly influenced by European modern art of the 1920s and 1930s, the example here, an early 1960s advertisement for a paper company, has its own personality attained through Rand's signature abstract marks and playful squiggles.

While the image may appear to be formless, it is deceptively disciplined. It takes a deft hand and a level of control to craft a collage that pulls the eye from one level of visual experience to the other while remaining cohesive. There is a carnivalesque abandon to the work that is anchored by his personal handwriting in the corner and freeform shapes. The most obvious binding element is colour – primary red, yellow and blue with black and white tying it all together, seemingly fortuitous yet, in fact, carefully composed. Collage is the result of improvisation, but it is also about the ability to know exactly when and where to stop.

⊠ Paul Rand, 1960
Advertisement for
the New York and
Pennsylvania paper
company

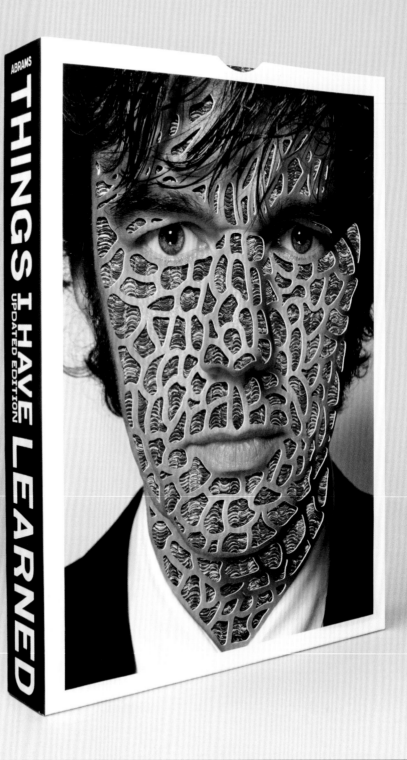

PAPER ART
Special Effects
in the Digital Age

Never underestimate the resiliency of paper. Despite predictions to the contrary, paper is not going the way of papyrus or parchment, and new and varied special paper effects are constantly keeping print design current.

Despite the migration to digital and online media for many old and new designed products, the range of weights, textures and colours is only matched by the variety of special effects (FX) that are possible when using paper – from slipsheets to pop-ups and tip-ins to embossing, die cuts and belly bands. Tactility is one of the best ways for analogue design to compete with digital media. Paper may not have the same luminosity as a screen page, but nonetheless it is fluid and tangible, easily moulded, transmuted and morphed into surprising and wondrous forms and formats.

The cover for Stefan Sagmeister's 2008 monograph *Things I Have Learned In My Life So Far* combines laser-cutting with traditional book-printing techniques in a portfolio format of special, individual booklets, each looking at a distinct project. It is a production and conceptual tour de force that reinvents the idea of a monograph. The booklets are housed in a slipcase that has been laser-cut in a lace-like pattern of Sagmeister's face. As the entire book is comprised of individual, removable booklets, each time one is detached a new design appears through the slipcase. It is not in the league of a fast-moving video game in terms of obsessive play, but it engages the eye and tests the imagination in a way that allows the reader to interact with the content at a personal pace.

Digital laser-cutting and other special-effect printing and binding tools have increased the viability of paper as a means to lure an audience into a graphically designed story or message. And who knows, paper just may be more durable and certainly more tangible than a purely digital or online experience.

⊠ Stefan Sagmeister, 2008
Things I Have Learned In My Life So Far book cover

MONUMENTALISM
The Bigger the Better

Graphic design is ostensibly flat but it is not always limited to two dimensions. Type and image can also exist off the printed page or screen, as an object in the environment. Environmental typography – the umbrella term for various indoor or outdoor announcements, commemorative inscriptions, wayfinding systems and public art – has a long history since ancient times. Today, environmental typography is as common on monuments as on billboards, on cornerstones and neon signs. Many of these environmental spectaculars represent Monumentalism, where type – either by itself or with imagery – is larger than life, with letterforms that are sculptural and grand.

In 1927 the Italian Futurist designer Fortunato Depero designed his 'Book Pavilion' – a temporary exhibition space for a publisher formed of concrete letters and words – at the Biennale Internazionale delle Arti Decorative in Monza. The mammoth letters were stacked like totem poles on the exterior and set as reliefs on the outer walls and roof. The building acted as an interactive billboard that beckoned people to enter, and showed that impactful type and architecture could function as a commercial tool.

A few years later, in 1931, Depero proposed a similar structure made of monumental letters for his client Campari. Although the structure was never realized, his preparatory sketches once again show the potential commercial impact of the concept – the combination of brand name with typographic scale and physicality is an advertising shot with a kick.

Monumentalism's greatest virtue is not that bigger is better, but that extreme exaggeration can create a sense of awe that will be remembered long after it has passed. Designers can simulate on paper or screen the impact of imposing type, while when accomplished in three-dimensional space – an exhibit, performance or stage set – typography can achieve monumental status.

⊠ Fortunato Depero, 1931
Preparatory sketch
for a proposed
structure for Campari

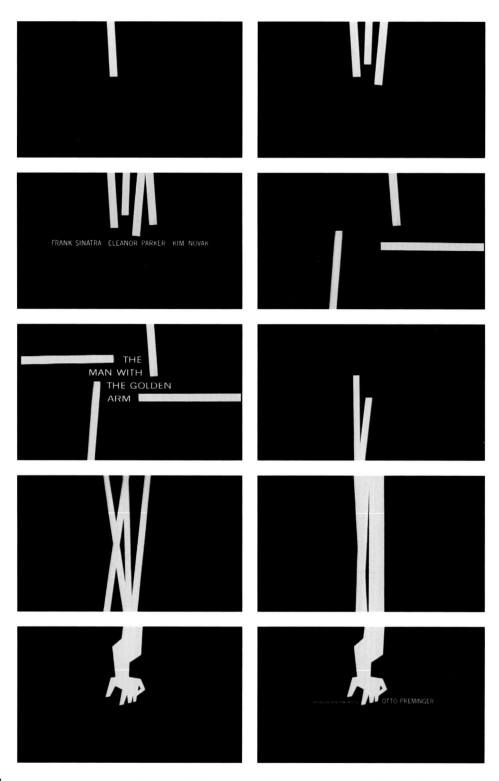

MOTION DESIGN
The Art of Kinetic Forms

Graphic design has embraced kinetic forms through digital technology, with a slew of new tools now available to the graphic designer to work with motion, sound, interactivity – and whatever comes next. Although these are distinct disciplines, their fairly recent embrace by new generations of graphic designers has essentially redefined the profession to include off-the-page experiences. Media platforms have increased as well and allow for better quality.

What graphic designers think of as motion design began in the early 1950s. Moving typography was among the earliest theatrical animations in films where type appears to move in sync with rhythmic music. This was later adopted by a few graphic designers who made typographic TV commercials. But type is not the only design element that can move – early expressionist films played with the movement of amorphous and geometric shapes and patterns. This is what Saul Bass was partially influenced by in his title sequence for the 1955 film *The Man with the Golden Arm*. The simple graphic reduces the plot about the struggles of a tormented heroin addict to a visual essence that expresses the film's emotional tension. Bass created a series of kinetic white bars on a black screen, which transformed into an abstract ballet of erratic shapes. After a few moments the bars became a twisted arm, a symbol of torment. It was an indelible graphic symbol – a logo, almost – which was equally effective for use in the print ad campaign.

The storyboard shown here is static, but is an example of how graphic design was used to tell a story when the technology made opticals time-consuming and expensive. It was a challenge to make something original, which makes these titles all the more noteworthy. With just these thumbnails it is possible to anticipate the moving version of the film, which set a standard at the time and still holds up.

⊠ Saul Bass, 1955
The Man with the Golden Arm film title sequence

USER-FRIENDLY DESIGN
Making New Ideas Accessible

The digital design world is a new realm in which the established conventions of graphic design form only part of the story. Aspects like time, motion, interaction, user experience and responsiveness, never considered twenty years ago, are now part of the mix. The virtual world can be more dynamic than the analogue one and active media offers many new ways to communicate by pushing ideas and information into the public domain.

This project by New York-based Control Group offers a virtual storefront for Amazon in the New York City subway system. Using a touch-and-swipe interface, individuals can browse products and have links and information sent from the kiosk to their phone or email account. According to Control Group the main challenge they faced was, 'how can we use design to make new interactions feel familiar?'

Without careful design choices, few passersby would expect to be able to interact with a digital advertisement, and fewer still would expect to be able to email or text themselves a product link from a subway platform. This led to the display of products in a grid of tiles that contained product images, names, prices and ratings – common on many conventional online storefronts. For this project, the design requirements were not to design a brand new, out-of-the-box interface but to exercise restraint and design an interface which offered simplistic familiarity.

During the late 1990s through the early 2000s, when some graphic designers were transitioning or incorporating digital experience into their practice, there was an anything-goes air of experimentation. The stakes are higher now that businesses such as Amazon depend on user-friendly applications to entice prospective audiences. Yet change is continual in this realm. What you learn or do today may easily change tomorrow. It is essential to keep abreast of invention and adapt design to it.

⊠ Control Group, 2014
Amazon digital
information kiosks

Borrow from design history

Karel Teige / Peter Bankov / Seymour Chwast / Marian Bantjes / Bertram Grosvenor Goodhue / Shepard Fairey / Copper Greene / Tibor Kalman / Art Chantry

ABSTRACTION
Leaving Room for Interpretation

Perceptions were forever altered when eastern European masters such as Wassily Kandinsky, František Kupka and Kazimir Malevich introduced non-figurative or abstract imagery into early twentieth-century art. No longer was what we saw what we got. Depictions of visual reality were unhinged and the ensuing changed perspectives and new styles opened the door to design and illustration that left room for interpretation. The aim of abstraction was to announce modernity – to be a benchmark of a new visual language. Adherents of traditional graphic design standards condemned abstraction as modern garbage best left on a canvas rather than a pristine graphically designed page, but eventually, with abstraction's acceptance throughout the design world in the form of mid-century Modernism, large numbers of designers could embrace its visual daring in their work.

Karel Teige's title page for *ZLOM*, a 1928 book of poems by Konstantin Biebl, abstracts the traditional nineteenth-century book layout in a rectilinear style of composition pioneered by the Russian Constructivists and practised by the Bauhaus. Teige, a member of the Czech avant-garde movement Zenit, used typecase materials, including metal 'furniture', printers' blocks and cuts, in what he referred to as 'typomontage'. Here, his abstract approach links the tone of the poetry to the typographic composition, proving that abstraction can be both interpretive and interpreted.

When working with abstract forms, a contemporary designer has the ability to capture a part of consciousness that refuses to accept conventions. When used smartly, to tease out a message, abstraction encourages the viewer to decipher and, therefore, connect with and remember what is deciphered.

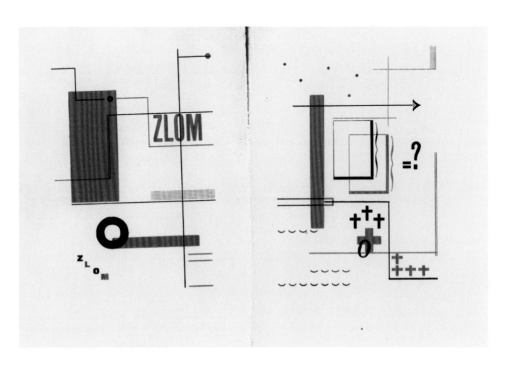

⊠ Karel Teige, 1928
ZLOM title page

EXPRESSIONISM
Achieving Shock and Awe

Expressionism in art takes reality and distorts it to communicate an emotionally charged or political message. As such, expressionism runs contrary to the tenets of neutral, universal or rational design – which is what the vast majority of designers are employed by their clients to deliver. Of course, a bit of rebellion is healthy and, when a message demands an emotive approach, looking to expressionistic styles is one way of achieving this.

Peter Bankov's poster for a lecture he gave at the New York Type Directors Club in 2014 is meant to be something of a self-portrait. Yet rather than a realistic depiction it is expressionistic – a representation of the inner Bankov. The scrawled and smeared drawing suggests an artist's mind in a child's body, a feeling that is heightened by the childlike, scribbled lettering declaring the designer's unbridled creativity – 'I make posters every day'. Each element of the piece is symbolically charged and full of energy, and seems to derive from the gut, not the brain alone. As Bankov's emotion runs rampant, his passion screams for attention.

Neo-expressionists take heed: this emotional approach can backfire if you're not careful. For instance, expressionism was used in 1990s design and illustration as a reaction against the slick, high-gloss work of the 1980s. In some instances, the rebellious style overpowered the intended message while at other times it *was* the intended message. The approach works when appearing unruly is the intention of the designer, not the consequence of making the wrong stylistic decision.

⊠ Peter Bankov, 2014
Type Directors Club
lecture poster

RETRO
Style as Tool

Retro refers to the borrowing of past design mannerisms to attract the attention of specific targeted audiences, whether for ironic effect, nostalgia or just plain stylishness. However, this is not just about using past styles as they were originally made but instead adapting them through the designer's imagination so that something new comes to the surface.

During the 1960s, Push Pin Studios in New York, founded by Seymour Chwast and Milton Glaser, 'quoted' and 'sampled' art nouveau and art deco to create the early incarnation of the world-renowned 'Push Pin Style'. Their studio attitude contradicted the prevailing mid-century Modernist dogma that the past should be rejected as a model for present and future. Push Pin combined their approach with an anti-modernist attitude that worked well in the areas of advertising, editorial and packaging.

Chwast's cover for the Jugendstil issue of *Design + Style*, a Mohawk Paper promotional series sampling historical styles, employs basic forms derived from German art nouveau, such as naturalistic ornament, curvilinear drawing and freeform lettering. But the intelligence is found in Chwast's wry sense of humour. For instance, the stylized cat is not borrowed from the past but reimagined for this publication – a wink and nod to the more serious applications of Jugendstil. And what could be wittier than a border made of little decorative Jugendstil mice? The graphic representations of geometric rodents are just the kind of deliberate goofiness that transcends mere copying and becomes true invention.

Designers use tropes from the past for pure aesthetic pleasure but they can also provide other cues or reference points that trigger memories or historical awareness. In this case, as the saying goes, 'It's the cat's meow'.

⊠ Seymour Chwast, 1986
Design + Style cover,
Jugendstil issue

I

WONDER

MARIAN BANTJES

The Monacelli Press

ORNAMENT
Gilding the Lily

The Modern architect Adolf Loos is often quoted for his 1908 essay 'Ornament is a Crime', in which he launched a caustic attack on the flourishes of late nineteenth-century art nouveau. In truth, though, ornamentation in graphic design is no more sinful or saintly than so-called purity – it is just about what kind of ornament is used and how well it is applied. The principal drawback of using ornament is that it usually conjures a certain time and place of conception; it can be fashionable or passé and clichéd, and it gets old fast.

Canadian designer Marian Bantjes has labelled the kneejerk adoption of mediocre decorative tropes 'uninteresting, mindless regurgitation of ornamental forms that has turned this aesthetic into a fad'. While she herself borrows heavily from the past, she has never been interested in recreating or emulating what has already been done. Rather she finds fresh opportunities in the juxtaposition of old and new and the 'paradoxes of content and style'. Ornament is part of this toolkit, but is used to maximize its aesthetic virtues rather than to promote nostalgic conceits.

The cover of Bantjes' first monograph, *I Wonder*, designed in 2010, evokes her passion for mathematically inspired ornamental intricacy. Although the influence is vintage, suggesting the Rococo style, the actual pattern is entirely her own design, deriving from deliberate reinterpretation of various formats.

Decorative excesses are the result of ignorant applications of anachronistic sampling from the past. However, there is a vast array of historical, contemporary and individually designed ornamentation to pique the fancy of any designer disposed to the style. When done well – and kept current through the designer's taste and skill – ornament frames and identifies a product or message while adding joy to the design experience.

⊠ Marian Bantjes, 2010
I Wonder book cover

FRAMES AND BORDERS
Experimenting with Graphic Relics

During the nineteenth century in Britain, lavish type and border treatments – referred to as 'artistic printing' – grew popular with the rise of consumerism. Advertisements, labels and packaging were all designed using typefaces and decoration in order to draw the eye and sell the product. As a result, Victorian commercial printers offered wider and wider selections of elaborate display typefaces, embellished borders and frames.

Inspirational books such as the William H. Page wood-type company's *Specimens of Chromatic Wood Type, Borders, Etc.* (1874), from which commercial printers could choose a wide selection of lavish decorative material, became bibles not only for late nineteenth- and early twentieth-century designers but for contemporary revivalists. Specimen books like these are today especially valuable for sampling the frames and borders that will evoke in contemporary work a sense of the past.

The border and illuminated capital shown here was designed in 1894 by American architect and type designer Bertram Grosvenor Goodhue, and is an example that is still relevant today. Its graphic power lies in the organic pattern that takes possession of the page and creates a window for the text to sit within. Of course there is an inescapable antique style at play, replete with exquisitely drafted images from nature and antiquity, which makes for an appealing vintage look.

Today, decorated frames and borders have a place as antidotes to the tyranny of the irrepressibly new and can be used, practically, to separate type and object on a page, to highlight and distinguish content, to use as elements in logos or monograms, and to develop other visual settings. All that's required is a little imagination and interpretation.

⊠ Bertram Grosvenor
Goodhue, 1894
Page from D.G. Rossetti's
The House of Life

☒ Shepard Fairey, 1992
Andre the Giant

☒ John Van Hamersveld,
1968
Jimi Hendrix

SAMPLING

Design as Tasting Menu

While a graphic designer can copy the great masters as a way of honing his or her craft, to determine how they did what they did, it's another story altogether to steal in order to derive creative or monetary profit from someone else's intellectual property. In graphic design, stealing is wrong, and copying is questionable. That said, sampling or appropriation is part of the artistic tradition.

Sampling began in music, with artists using a portion of another's recordings as a form of experimentation. In graphic design, quoting a portion of someone else's image is, perhaps, ethically questionable, but it is accepted that design is an interaction that uses common ideas to convey a message or tell a story. Sometimes this is most efficiently communicated through the familiar pictorial language of another designer's work.

American street artist Shepard Fairey spent a large part of his early career mastering a form of sampling in which he transformed his own character, Andre the Giant (itself a sample, since Andre was a real wrestler), into other guises. John Van Hamersveld's vintage 1968 Jimi Hendrix poster is one of Fairey's acknowledged inspirations. In 1992, when Fairey made his version of the image, skateboard culture's use of irreverent appropriation and subversion was at its peak, with logos and brands being pirated and transformed with salacious yet witty names. Fairey's piece is less a parody – that is, done for comic effect – than a celebration of and homage to the original, recreating its style by retaining the basic format, font and colours, but with an added twist.

Reasons for designers to sample include experimentation – using segments of existing works to create another – and commentary, to examine what the original work represents. Clarity of purpose is useful if sampling is accomplished, so that it doesn't cross over the line into stealing.

Borrow from Design History

PARODY
Balancing Recognition with Surprise

Parody in graphic design is a form of visual satire that mimics recognizable pictorial iconography, from brand logos to works of art, to humorously comment on something significant. Parody only succeeds if the audience is familiar with the object of parody and when they see the connection. It can be strident or silly. If the humour is sharp, parody can be both informative and entertaining.

In 2003 Apple advertised its iPod with a series of posters showing a dancer wearing the emblematic white iPod earphones, silhouetted against a vibrant colour field. The arresting print campaign was in such wide circulation that it was ripe for parody. This came in 2004 after photographic revelations of torture at the US military prison in Abu Ghraib, Iraq, were leaked to the press. Arguably the most abhorrent of these was of a detainee in a hood and poncho standing on a box with electrical wires attached to his body. The shockwave of these images hit the American public hard.

By way of protest, New York artists collective Copper Greene recast the horrifying image as a spot-on parody of the iPod posters. It showed the tortured victim wearing the eerie hood against a bright purple colour field with white electrical wires attached to his hands. In perfect guerilla style, the collective's designers posted this protest poster alongside the iPod posters on New York hoardings, adding fuel to the growing criticism of the occupation of Iraq.

One of the most clever and memorable parodies ever produced, the image certainly touched a chord, and for good reason it is among the most well-known and widely circulated protest posters of the decade. All the components are in alignment, down to the most nuanced detail, including the exact iPod font, colours, manipulation of image – and especially the emblematic white wires, another mnemonic highlight. Such attention to detail is what separates a memorable graphic parody from a simple joke or gag.

⊠ Copper Greene, 2004
iRaq

NOVEMBER

SOUP   BOUDIN & WARM TARTS

GUSTY WINDS

HIGH S UPPER 40S TO MID 50S

LOWS UPPER 30S TO MID 40S

FLORENT

OPEN 24 HOURS 989 5779

WATCH FOR HEAVY RAINS

WEAR YOUR GALOSHES

MNCO

VERNACULAR
Everyday Aesthetics

In today's graphic design practice, the word 'vernacular' signifies a stylistic interest in run-of-the-mill commercial arts, including laundry tickets, cheese labels, road signs, cigarette boxes, sweet wrappers, restaurant menus, and other everyday products and by-products of industry and commerce. Unlike true folk art, which is created by the untutored, these are studied commercial artefacts that document shifting states of mass communication over the years.

The vernacular 'movement' in design began in the early 1970s, when figures such as the architect Robert Venturi proposed that commercial detritus, with its 'forgotten symbolism', could be beautiful. In 1985, for the branding of the quirky Restaurant Florent, a former diner located in the then-seedy Meatpacking district of Manhattan, Hungarian-born designer Tibor Kalman and his firm M&Co used the classic changeable letter board found in most common diners and coffee shops, complete with typical misspellings.

In this context, vernacular was a logical response to the location and look of the physical space of the restaurant, with its Formica tables, bar stools and stainless-steel counter and appliances. Yet it was shocking for its time. Designers were comfortable using nineteenth-century vernacular typefaces, but the 1940s and 1950s were still off-limits for appropriation. Kalman opened the doors to a restaurant that reacted against 1980s culture and politics, and his design scheme was part and parcel of its appeal.

The vernacular style works when there is a bit of knowing irony. Kalman and his client believed that this down-to-earth approach, with its subtle wink and nod, would have great appeal to those who wanted something hip but not pretentious. Have fun with vernacular but be careful not to use it where it does not belong.

⊠ Tibor Kalman, 1985
Branding for Restaurant
Florent, New York

Borrow from Design History

VINTAGE EPHEMERA
Making Eyesores
Look Good

In all forms of design, if you wait long enough, good eventually becomes bad and bad somehow looks better than ever. As with vernacular, a designer somewhere is always going to dig up a style from the past and make it fashionable in the present. Whether or not the results could truly be considered 'great graphic design' is a subjective judgement, but many times over the past decades design, type and illustration once deemed eyesores have been turned into eye-catchers – it just takes a spirit of enterprise.

Seattle designer Art Chantry built his career around taking rudimentary commercial art – the so-called 'showcard' genre of hand-painted and roughly printed adverts or posters used to publicize everything from carnivals to drive-ins and motor parts – and making it into something else. Part parody, part homage, during the late 1980s and 1990s Chantry designed hundreds of grunge and other indie rock music concert posters and record sleeves. At the time, even in their vintage guise, his posters were fresh to the audience of kids that embraced them. There was an air of whimsy in some and comedy in others. This poster, using the souped-up graphics of horror movies and carnival midways, is for a rock concert whose audience would understand and appreciate the visual references.

Although some formalist graphic designers probably gag at the thought of tawdry 'anti design', this genre opens the door to appropriate virtually any graphic style and, as such, provides an opportunity to create exciting work. Designing with printed ephemera also gives an instant vintage charm that holds great appeal for the audiences that buy into the music and fashion it represents. The urge to copy Chantry's method might outweigh the need to be cautious. The approach has its limitations but when understood it can result in a catchy piece of work.

⊠ Art Chantry, 1997
The Cramps poster

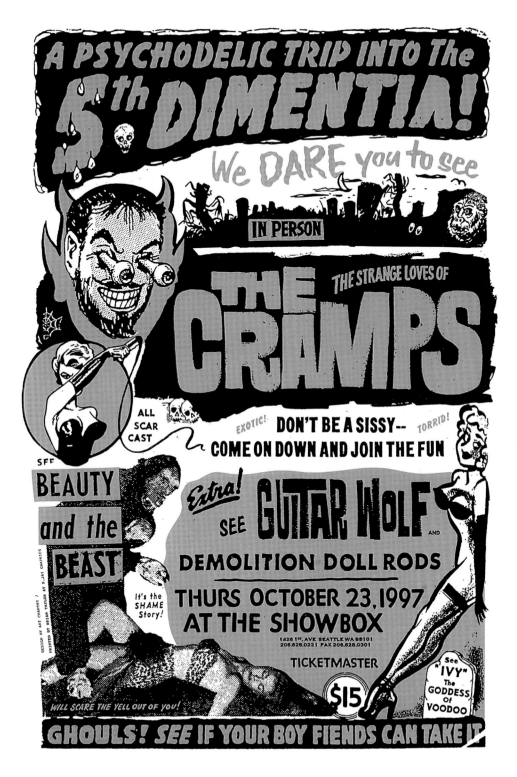

Communicate a message

AG Fronzoni / Gerd Arntz / Otl Aicher / Abram Games / Steff Geissbuhler / Paul Sahre / Massin / Michael Schwab / John Heartfield / Christoph Niemann

SIMPLICITY
Less is More

———————— **Getting rid of extraneous design matter enables the viewer to focus on the essential message of a particular visual communication. This is an aesthetic thought to originate from the German Bauhaus in the 1920s, following an epoch of excessive stylized ornament in the form of art nouveau. The Modernist mantra 'Less is more', credited to the architect Ludwig Mies van der Rohe, remains as true today as it did in the early twentieth century.**

In 1896 simplicity in the world of graphic design emerged when a young German poster artist, Lucian Bernhard, invented the *Sachplakat* (object poster). His prototype Priester Match poster of 1906 used bright colours and a pared-down composition to create an unfettered visual advertising message on a par with a logo.

Italian minimalist designer AG Fronzoni's 1979 poster *I manifesti di Michele Spera* offers a different kind of simplicity, not *Sachplakat* per se, but a modern expansion of the concept in which – rather than focusing on an object – type and image are combined in a minimal manner. The poster advertises the work of another modern Italian graphic designer, with the linear component suggesting the first letter of Spera's last name, without manifesting a literal S. The grid is economical and enables the rectangles to outline the central point in the poster. The type is flush left, ragged right on the central axis, anchored in white space and providing an elegant readability.

Simplicity signals utility, clarity and sophistication, while minimalism is similar, but more dogmatic and formulaic. To achieve great design, do not consider clutter as an impediment but reduce the text and image so it is functional – legible and readable – and retain those minimal qualities that will ensure the message will be received.

⊠ AG Fronzoni, 1979
I manifesti di Michele Spera exhibition poster

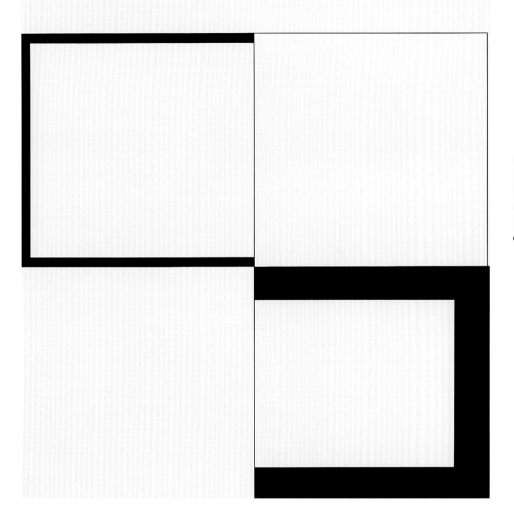

10-21 maggio 1979
I manifesti di Michele Spera
Teatro del falcone
Comune di Genova
Assessorato alla cultura

SYMBOLS OF PICTORIAL STATISTICS

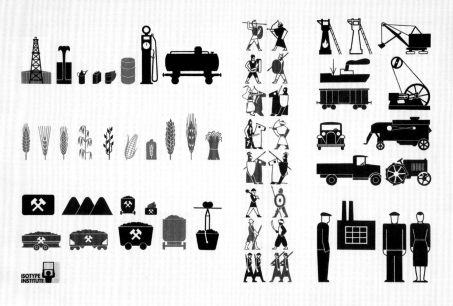

INFORMATION GRAPHICS
Clarify with Simple Pictures

The most significant change in twenty-first-century graphic design has been the rise of information graphics, also known as data visualization. The flood of information, speed of dissemination and demand for interpretation generated by the internet have created a profound need for clarification. Graphic designers have to be skilled at translating facts and figures into accessible graphic components.

The practice of turning data into visual charts, graphs and maps began before the twentieth century, but it was in the 1920s that it became a democratizing movement among Modernist designers. The exemplar symbol maker, German Modernist commercial artist and designer Gerd Arntz, synthesized categories of data, such as population, literacy and fuel consumption, into groups of graphic icons that were given numerical values to enable visual reading of complex information. These are still commonly used today, and in roughly the same form as when Arntz worked with Otto Neurath to design the Isotype system between 1925 and 1934.

Isotype (International System of Typographic Picture Education) was created as a 'world language without words', used to unify people of many languages. The graphical elements were as reductive as possible without being confusingly abstract. With a vernacular familiarity – people understand them because of their ubiquity – these symbols have become a kind of universal language. Today many printed and online editorial media regularly use infographics as an alternative to lengthy written stories, exactly because they want to help readers consume relevant data quickly.

Purists would say that you should only use infographics for a data-driven piece, but that is too rigid. Infographics can be used as an entry point into an article or as a focal point on a poster; they can be quirky and eccentric, yet relevant too. Infographics can reduce the stress of information overload and help the reader feel more secure with what they do know.

⊠ Gerd Arntz and
Otto Neurath, 1925
*Symbols of Pictorial
Statistics*

Communicate a Message

SYMBOLS

Writing Long with Graphic Shorthand

Symbols, icons, and lately emoticons and emoji are popular shorthand used to convey everything from broad concepts to short phrases through visual linguistics. They are written and gestural language rolled into one. Used for diagrams and signs, and in social media, they are more popular than ever because of their centrality in the digital ecosystem. As the appeal of social media has grown – and graphic designers have become inextricably involved in its creation – emoticons, used since the 1980s, and emoji, first introduced in Japan in the late 1990s, offer ways to incorporate tone or gestures into communication, and serve as a substitute for conventional forms of address.

There is, however, a danger that graphic symbols will become fashionable and cloying clichés (think of the happy face), so designers are routinely inventing new ones. Yet as much as symbol mania has caught on, it is important to remember when developing symbols that clear transmission is a crucial virtue of the form. While there are many fine examples, such as the work of Gerd Arntz, the elegant symbol system created by German designer Otl Aicher for the 1972 Munich Olympics is the model of them all.

Aicher's set of pictograms was so exquisitely precise and rational because they were based entirely on geometry, grids and the typeface Univers 55. As a result, void of racial or ethnic characteristics, they are still models of effective multilingual and multicultural design. As a system of identity they are striking indicators that have personality yet universality.

Not all symbol systems are as fluent and fluid as Aicher's pictograms – which is fine, as long as they carry the message – but all attempts at pictographic design should function as effective shorthand rather than decorative indulgence.

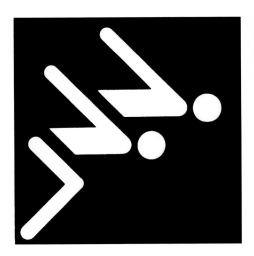

⊠ Otl Aicher, 1972
Munich Olympics
symbol system

TARGETING

Take Aim, Design for Reaction

Graphic design has the ability to command, advocate, educate – in short, to force the viewer into changing their feelings and behaviour. In order to do this you need to mix precise ingredients of word and picture, which involves choosing the most demonstrative typeface to stand alone or together with a memorable image. With the right elements, a poster, book cover or brochure can elicit both a physical and an emotional reaction. It is a force not to be taken lightly.

British graphic designer Abram Games' World War II poster *Your Talk May Kill Your Comrades* packs a double-whammy punch. The way the title is styled over two lines, singling out 'Your Talk', breaks the cadence of the slogan so that the message is aimed at 'you', while separating out 'Talk May Kill' in white emphasizes the textual warning. Visually, the concentric circles of death emanating from the soldier's mouth incriminate him as both a launch pad and target of wrongdoing. The coiled spear that grows out from those circles echoes the blood-red tint in the word 'your' and takes on a snake-like appearance, subliminally suggesting that the speaker is a viper. The coup de grâce, the three soldiers speared to death, underscores how serious loose lips can be – three men representing many more.

Games' poster, one of many he created for the war effort, is arguably one of the most powerful cautionary, targeted messages of the entire war. When all the communicative components are in sync, the impact on your audience can make them stop, look and react.

⊠ Abram Games, 1942
Your Talk May Kill Your Comrades

PERSUASION
A Sign That Commands

There is no better example of human interaction with a graphic symbol and message than the universal stop sign. The red field and white letters are an instant message conveyor that invariably triggers a behavioural response – the essence of interaction.

The stop sign is one of many ways that the process of informing can result in action. There are scores of examples where typography and visuals project equally strong messages. One is Swiss-born Steff Geissbuhler's cautionary poster, which draws on the equity of the stop sign's ubiquity, and the appropriation of the iconic hexagon shape in red and white as the platform for the word 'AIDS' in striking Gothic type.

Not all visual commands to stop, go or pursue have to follow the same formula as Geissbuhler's, but this mode of communication already has a tried and tested recognizability. While this is a pun of sorts, it also gives the clearest message responding to the worldwide epidemic. The emotional resonance of this familiar plea motivates the viewer to engage.

Of course the bigger question is the effectiveness of any poster advocating eradication. This clearly says STOP AIDS and as graphic design it has a high level of conceptual sophistication and is a good model for designers to use existing signs to underscore certain advocacy messages. But don't place a lot of hope in a single image to save the world. What this poster does well is to create awareness. It is an emblem of hope and banner of battle, and in this sense it is great design for what it can accomplish.

⊠ Steff Geissbuhler, 1989
STOP AIDS!

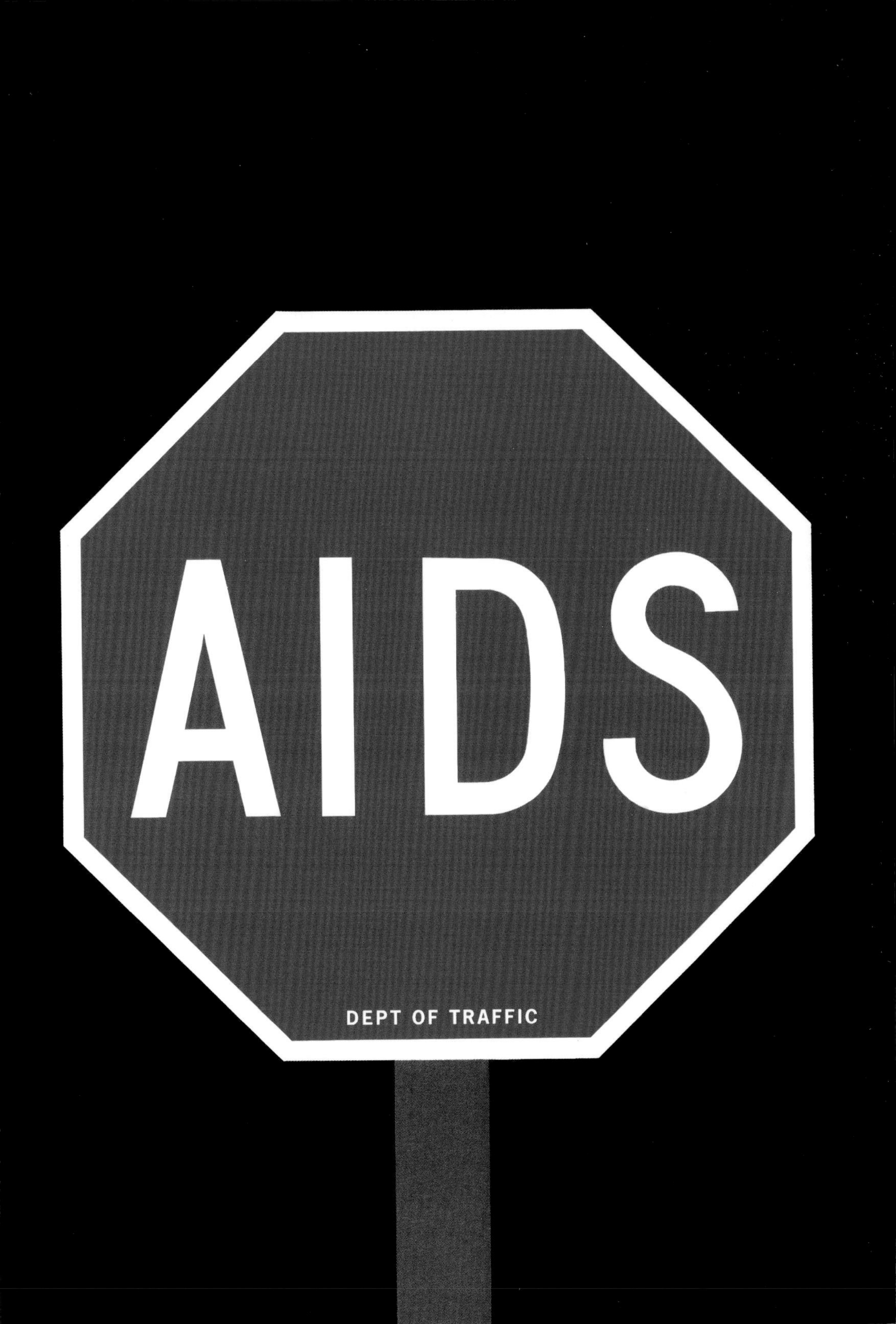
AIDS
DEPT OF TRAFFIC

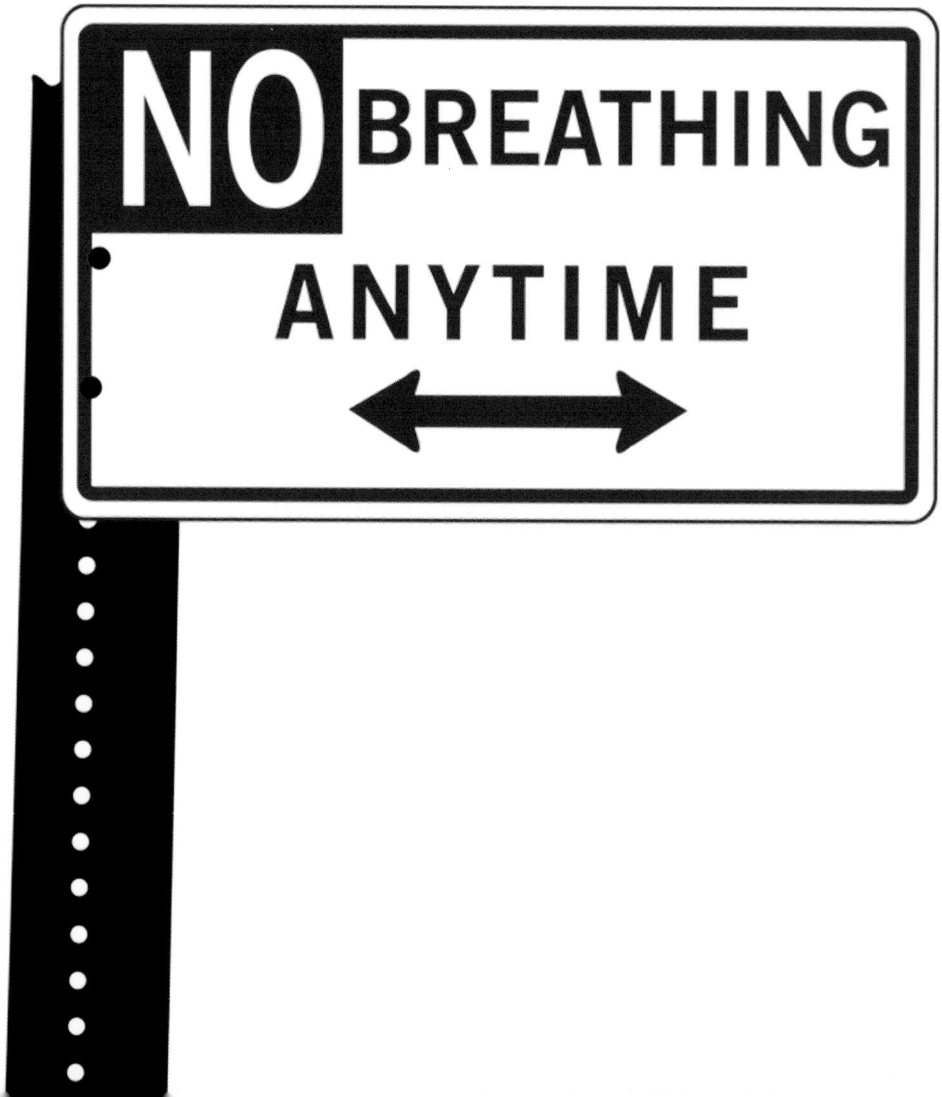
NO BREATHING
ANYTIME

GRAPHIC COMMENTARY
Social Critique through Satirical Design

Historically, type and image have played a huge role in sociopolitical discourse by way of commentary and critique. Whether commissioned by a client or self-initiated, graphic commentary in the form of posters, placards, billboards, advertisements and other media serves to illuminate, provoke and sometimes instigate activity for or against an issue or cause. When employing wit and irony to make a political or social statement of purpose, designers have the capacity to alter behaviour or, at the very least, make people think. They also have the ability to make people mad through type and imagery that provokes negative as well as positive emotions.

Provocation is as much an outcome of graphic commentary as an intention. New York designer Paul Sahre's transformation of a common parking sign into a tool of social critique shows how quoting and twisting familiar iconography can result in an astonishingly sardonic message. Sahre created this piece to illustrate a story in *The New York Times* about the confusing and frustrating New York City parking regulations. Having had his car dragged down to the pound on more than one occasion, Sahre derived great satisfaction from making and publishing this illustration. Personal involvement in a piece of graphic social or political criticism like this gives the work grit, while connecting on a familiar level with the audience.

A visual idea has even greater merit when its relevance reaches beyond its original purpose. As well as being a comment on confusing signage, Sahre's sign also addresses larger environmental concerns about clean air in urban places. The intelligence of this design solution is evident in its two interpretations for the price of one. Sahre's piece strikes a balance between the client's message and the designer's personal motivation: while it illustrates the commissioned editorial concept, it says a lot more on top.

⊠ Paul Sahre, 2003
No Breathing Anytime

NARRATIVE
Visual Storytelling

Every layout tells a story. Graphic design can manipulate the elements of visual communication – type and image – to lead the reader or viewer from one scene, concept or thought to another, both in linear and circuitous ways. Think of the reader as a driver, who is free to slow down or speed up at will, but who is guided by the designer with speed bumps and traffic signs in the form of type and image size, scale and style.

The best examples of this process are found in editorial media – books and magazines – where the act of turning pages is a journey through space and time. Web pages and apps are even larger platforms for building narrative, using the same page-turning metaphor.

Such an enhanced narrative layout is key to the work of French author and designer Massin, whose first and most famous leap into design authorship was his distinctive 1964 interpretation of Eugène Ionesco's surrealist play *The Bald Soprano*. Here Massin created the prototype of a kinetic storyboard. His method was simple: give each character a typographic equivalent of their voice by assigning them their own typeface – with its own size, weight and orientation – and illustrate each voice with a high-contrast photograph of the cast.

Massin's work perfectly integrates word and picture in a compelling way that invites the reader to virtually experience Ionesco's play by reading along and turning the pages. While this is a unique example of pictorial narrative flow, the technique is applicable for all kinds of books for adults and children where type and image are dynamically integrated. Its impact is similar to that of reading a graphic novel.

ouvrent tout grand la bouche

ah ! oh ! oh ! oh ! allons de dents

laissez-moi grincer caïman

Ulysse

je n'en vais habiter ma

cagn dans, me cacaoyers

les cacaoyers des cacao donnent des cacahuètes donnent du cacao !

les cacaoyers des cacao donnent pas des cacahuètes donnent du cacao !

les cacaoyers

☒ Massin, 1964
Spread from *The
Bald Soprano*

MOOD
Set the Tone
through Nuance

There are a number of ways in which a designer can evoke the mood of a piece. Colour triggers certain responses: yellow, orange and green suggest happiness or hopefulness while the darker red, purple and black conjure more sombre feelings. Type styles also set a stage: lightweight sans-serif type appears less serious than a medium-weight serif face, while extra-bold sans serifs can give an in-your-face sense of foreboding. Illustration and photography can also contribute. Mood is most effectively captured through nuance, a host of subtle visual gestures that push our perceptual buttons.

There are many reasons why Michael Schwab's 1995 cover for *The Gettin Place* by Susan Straight, a novel dealing with American race riots and the impact of violence on three generations of a family, establishes the mood of the book so poignantly. The deep red that fills the background signals a dramatic plot, while the black figures stand for a family steeped in a shadowy past. The scant blue-grey in the shirt, face and glasses – while introducing a touch of light – also heightens the reader's anticipation of the tale waiting to unfold. The stance of the figures all facing different ways evokes conflict or doubt, complemented by the lettering, which infers a tentative sensibility. When viewed together the components give the uneasy feeling that something is about to occur. The cover was created shortly after the digital revolution, but Schwab chose to draw the image and then scan it into Photoshop to achieve a more dramatic effect. The mood is sombre but not offputting. While the visual elements suggest sadness there is also beauty in the composition – and that's the balance that must be maintained.

Establishing mood through graphic design and illustration requires using a variety of tools subtly, as here. When first seen, the image evokes a strong feeling, but the elements that contribute to that feeling are only evident when the work is deconstructed piece by piece.

⊠ Michael Schwab, 1995
The Gettin Place
book cover

Communicate a Message

EMOTION
Passion for Your Subject

There has always been an understanding that graphic designers should express their passions in their personal art and not their commercially paid work. Individual style was not *verboten*, but a client's message was not an appropriate platform – unless it was at the client's own request – for personal commentary. Nonetheless, designers are often wired to convey emotion through their illustrative and typographic output. Emotion is not a style and should be used respectfully and intelligently, when the subject demands it. True emotion-based design demands a buzz between designer and subject.

One of the most emotionally charged designs of the twentieth century is John Heartfield's 1928 German national election poster for the Communist party titled *The Hand Has Five Fingers*. It shows a silhouetted soiled, raised hand, presumably that of a worker, with his fingers splayed as though he were desperately grabbing at something out of reach – victory at the polls against the Nazi party.

Using the hand to represent ordinary individuals working together is at once a daring yet recognizable image. Daring because it's not what is expected on a typical election poster (it puts the voter rather than the politician centre stage), and recognizable because every voter understands the reference on a visceral level. When seen on the street individually or in rows of three or more, the hand or hands appear to grab the hearts and minds of the passersby, breaking through the visual clutter of an election campaign.

The designer who sets out to create something that qualifies as emotional is certain to fail. The feeling that emerges from a poster like this is not programmed but rather a consequence of the designer's commitment to the message and the idea.

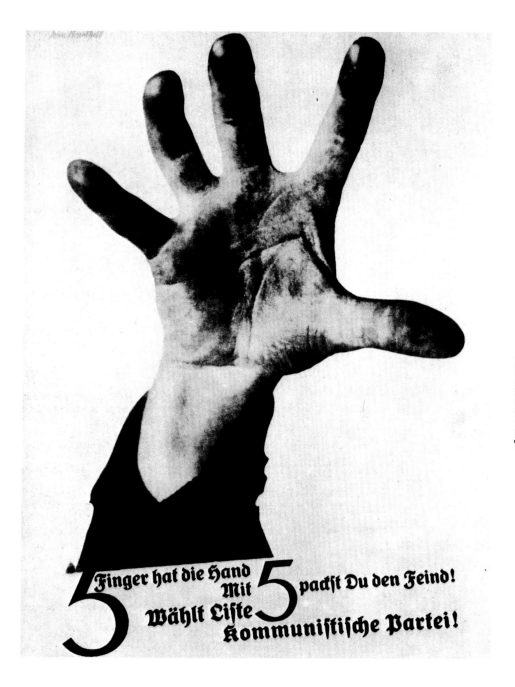

⊠ John Heartfield, 1928
The Hand Has
Five Fingers

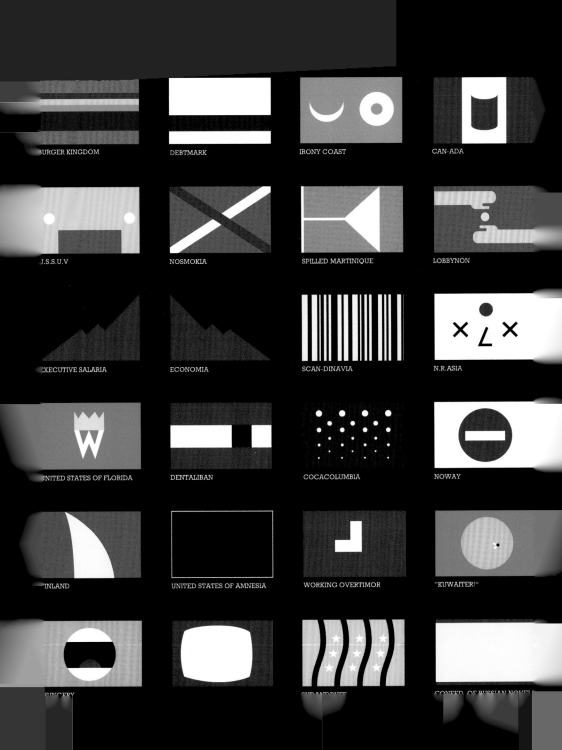

BURGER KINGDOM

DEBTMARK

IRONY COAST

CAN-ADA

U.S.S.U.V

NOSMOKIA

SPILLED MARTINIQUE

LOBBYNON

EXECUTIVE SALARIA

ECONOMIA

SCAN-DINAVIA

N.R.ASIA

UNITED STATES OF FLORIDA

DENTALIBAN

COCACOLUMBIA

NOWAY

FINLAND

UNITED STATES OF AMNESIA

WORKING OVERTIMOR

"KUWAITER!"

HUNGERY

SUDANDRUFF

CONTED OF RUSSIAN NOVEL

WIT AND HUMOUR
Tickle the Funny Bone

As a selling tool, humour in graphic design acts as a hook to grab attention and entice the viewer into the message. Humour used in this way can't be too outrageous, lest the purpose be defeated. Entire books have been written about design and humour because it has been proven that wit engages all the cognitive and physical senses of the viewer. The designer can therefore tap into all kinds of humour, whether instinctive or deliberate, to communicate, inform, entertain and manipulate.

While humour can be a lure, it is best when it is offered as an extra dollop of enjoyment for the viewer. It can also be a 'spoonful of sugar to help the medicine go down' for the designer in an otherwise sleep-inducing assignment – and is this really so bad? No precise formula exists for how or when to be funny, so you could argue that almost any project can be considered fair game for the designer (though of course they don't all invite humour). Using humour in design is an art, not a set of rules.

Some designers are just naturally witty, like Berlin-based Christoph Niemann, whose 2004 work *The Real Empires of Evil* provides a hilariously thought-provoking satirical survey of the flags of mythical regimes. This is a stand-alone piece commissioned by *Nozone* magazine, rather than a response to a design brief, so the humour is not self-conscious but instead has a quirky uninhibitedness, which enables a personal viewpoint to emerge. The clever match-ups – like 'Noway', with a flag resembling a Japanese rising sun as a Dead End sign, and 'Can-ada', with a can in place of a maple leaf – force a double take. The colourful grid of geometric and abstract rectangles brings a smile to the eye and pleasure to the brain.

Too much forethought can kill a visual joke, but refinement is essential. When making an intentionally witty piece of work, make sure it is really funny: put it aside for an hour and then look again with fresh eyes.

⊠ Christoph Niemann, 2004
The Real Empires of Evil

Communicate a Message

GLOSSARY

Art deco A distinctly 'modern' international art and design movement of the 1920s that began in Europe and spread throughout the industrialized world.

Art nouveau A major turn-of-the-century art and design movement and style known for its naturalistic ornamentation and excessive use of tendrils and vines.

Avant-garde Designation given to progressive art or design groups, movements and methods that challenge conventional practice.

Baroque A style of European art and design of the 17th and 18th centuries that fostered ornate detail.

Bauhaus State-sponsored German design school (1919–33), known as one of the wellsprings of modern design and typography. Closed in 1933 by the Nazis.

Blackletter Gothic-script lettering used by medieval scribes that served as the basis for Gutenberg's original metal typefaces. Once considered the German national type style.

Central axis composition Classic style of page composition in which lines of text are centred on the page rather than *flush* left or right.

CMYK The process colours used in printing full-colour reproductions: Cyan, Magenta, Yellow and Black.

Constructivist An art and design movement and style that originated in Russia from the 1917 Revolution, which rejected the idea of 'art for art's sake' in favour of art serving a social purpose. Stylistically known for asymmetrical type compositions, heavy bars, no ornament and limited colour.

Cubist A revolutionary way of creating representations in which objects are analyzed, broken up and reassembled in an abstract form. Pioneered by Pablo Picasso and Georges Braque, it was adopted by graphic designers as a stylistic mannerism to express modernity.

Curvilinear Fluid forms in *art nouveau* which are rooted in the intersection and intertwining of meandering lines; the opposite of rectilinear or angular lines.

Die cuts A printing production technique wherein a die is used to cut shapes, lines or letters out of paper.

Embossing A printing production technique where the impression of shapes, lines or letters is recessed into paper.

Emoji Symbolic digital icons that come in many styles and forms and are used to express a wide range of concepts and emotions, including anger, awe, sadness and joy.

Emoticons Similar to *emoji*, but more primitive and with less emotional range and visual style.

Flush left, ragged right Type composed in lines that are lined up or *justified* on the left but not on the right.

Futurist A radical art and design movement started in Italy in 1909. Futurist typography was know as '*parole in libertà*' (words in freedom), characterized by words composed to represent noise and speech.

Gothic type The term and family for *sans-serif* typefaces. Can also refer to *blackletter* type.

Instagram Digital photo-sharing app that has become popular on social media.

Jugendstil The German form of *art nouveau* practised by designers, typographers and cartoonists.

Justified text Typography that is lined up (*flush*) on both sides, not *ragged* right or left.

Legibility The relative ease with which type and image are read; see also *readability.*

Mnemonic As described by Paul Rand, the component of an otherwise ordinary design intended to be a memorable cue, like the parallel lines of the IBM logo.

Modernism The overarching rubric for a radical early to mid-twentieth-century transformative art and design movement that overturned conventions and continues to have influence. Included under this rubric are the Bauhaus, Constructivism and Futurism.

Photogram A photographic image made without a camera by placing objects directly onto the surface of a light-sensitive material. This method was popularized by Man Ray and frequently used in Modernist design.

Pica For printers and designers, a unit of type size and line length equal to 12 points (about a sixth of an inch or 4.2 mm).

Pop-ups A complicated but common printing special effect whereby flat elements on a page surface become dimensional when the spread is opened.

Ragged right See *flush left, ragged right.*

Readability Similar to *legibility*, but something can be 'read' or understood without having to be completely legible. Deciphering a stylistic code that is illegible can produce readability.

Rebus A manifestation whereby pictures are substituted to represent words or parts of words.

Rococo An eighteenth-century artistic movement and style known, like *Baroque*, for excessive ornament.

Sachplakat German for 'object poster'; simplified but effective advertising posters that use only the product name and a stylized representation of the product itself.

Sans serif Type without *serifs* at the bottom of letters.

Serifs The variously sized and weighted baselines at the bottom of letters that derive from the flared stroke at the ends of Roman (Latin) inscriptional letters.

Slipcase In book production, the outer envelope or box that encases a book and its cover.

Slipsheet An unbound sheet of paper in a book or publication that separates two pages from one another.

Start caps Also called 'initial caps' and 'drop caps', these are enlarged letters used to indicate the beginning of a new chapter, section or paragraph. When ornate they are called illuminated initials.

Swiss Style A design movement that began in the 1950s, which advocated severe limitations on type, colour, picture and ornament, with the goal of legibility, functionality and unfettered readability.

Tip-ins In printing, separate printed pieces that are glued or otherwise attached to bound pages.

FURTHER READING

GENERAL DESIGN

Albrecht, Donald, Ellen Lupton and Steven Holt. *Design Culture Now: National Design Triennial* (New York: Princeton Architectural Press, 2000).

Anderson, Gail. *Outside the Box: Hand-Drawn Packaging from Around the World* (New York: Princeton Architectural Press, 2015).

Bass, Jennifer and Pat Kirkham. *Saul Bass: A Life in Film and Design* (London: Laurence King Publishing, 2011).

Bierut, Michael, William Drenttel, Steven Heller and D.K. Holland, eds. *Looking Closer: Critical Writings on Graphic Design* (New York: Allworth, 1994).

Blackwell, Lewis, ed. *The End of Print: The Graphic Design of David Carson* (San Francisco: Chronicle Books, 1996).

Bringhurst, Robert. *The Elements of Typographic Style* (Vancouver: Hartley & Marks, 2004).

Elam, Kimberly. *Grid Systems: Principles of Organizing Type* (New York: Princeton Architectural Press, 2004).

Erler, J., ed. *Hello, I am Erik: Erik Spiekerman, Typographer, Designer, Entrepreneur* (Berlin: Gestalten, 2014).

Helfland, Jessica. *Screen: Essays on Graphic Design, New Media, and Visual Culture* (New York: Princeton Architectural Press, 2004).

Heller, Steven and Gail Anderson. *Typographic Universe: Letterforms Found in Nature, the Built World and Human Imagination* (London/New York: Thames & Hudson, 2014).

Heller, Steven and Véronique Vienne. *100 Ideas That Changed Graphic Design* (London: Laurence King Publishing, 2012).

Heller, Steven and Seymour Chwast. *Graphic Style: From Victorian to Digital* (New York: Harry N. Abrams, 2001).

Heller, Steven. *Graphic Style Lab* (Boston: Rockport Press, 2015).

Heller, Steven. *Paul Rand* (London: Phaidon Press, 1999).

Heller, Steven and Véronique Vienne. *Becoming a Graphic and Digital Designer* (New York: Wiley & Sons, 2015).

Heller, Steven and Louise Fili. *Stylepedia: A Guide to Graphic Design Mannerisms, Quirks, and Conceits* (San Francisco: Chronicle Books, 2006).

Heller, Steven and Louise Fili. *Typology: Type Design from the Victorian Era to the Digital Age* (San Francisco: Chronicle Books, 1999).

Heller, Steven and Mirko Ilić. *The Anatomy of Design: Uncovering the Influences and Inspirations in Modern Graphic Design* (Rockport, MA: Rockport, 2007).

Heller, Steven. *The Education of a Typographer* (New York: Allworth, 2004).

Heller, Steven. *Handwritten: Expressive Lettering in the Digital Age* (New York/London: Thames & Hudson, 2004).

Heller, Steven. *Design Literacy: Understanding Graphic Design* (New York: Allworth, 2014).

Hollis, Richard. *Graphic Design: A Concise History* (*World of Art* series), 2nd edn (New York/London: Thames & Hudson, 2001).

Lipton, Ronnie. *The Practical Guide to Information Design* (New York: John Wiley & Sons, Inc., 2007).

Lupton, Ellen. *How Posters Work* (New York: Cooper Hewitt, Smithsonian Design Museum, 2015).

Lupton, Ellen. *Thinking with Type: A Critical Guide for Designers, Writers, Editors and Students* (New York: Princeton Architectural Press, 2004).

McAlhone, Beryl et al. *A Smile in the Mind: Witty Thinking in Graphic Design* (London: Phaidon Press, 1998).

Maeda, John. *Maeda @ Media* (London/New York: Thames & Hudson, 2000).

Meggs, Philip B. and Alston Purvis. *A History of Graphic Design*, 4th edn (New York: John Wiley & Sons, 2006).

Munari, Bruno. *Design as Art* (New York: Penguin, 2008).

Poynor, Rick. *No More Rules: Graphic Design and Postmodernism* (New Haven, CT: Yale University Press, 2003).

Rand, Paul. *Thoughts on Design* (San Francisco: Chronicle Books, repr. 2014).

Sagmeister, Stefan and Peter Hall. *Made You Look* (New York: Booth-Clibborn, 2001).

Samara, Timothy. *Making and Breaking the Grid: A Graphic Design Layout Workshop* (Rockport, MA: Rockport, 2005).

Shaughnessy, Adrian. *How To Be a Graphic Designer Without Losing Your Soul* (New York: Princeton Architectural Press, 2005).

Sinclair, Mark. *TM: The Untold Stories Behind 29 Classic Logos* (London: Laurence King Publishing, 2014).

Thorgerson, Storm and Aubrey Powell. *100 Best Album Covers* (London/New York/Sydney: Dorling Kindersley, 1999).

Twemlow, Alice. *What is Graphic Design For?* (London: RotoVision, 2006).

DIGITAL DESIGN

Ellison, Andy. *The Complete Guide to Digital Type: Creative Use of Typography in the Digital Arts* (London: Collins, 2004).

Goux, Melanie and James Houff. *On Screen In Time: Transitions in Motion Graphic Design for Film, Television and New Media* (London: RotoVision, 2003).

Greene, David. *Motion Graphics (How Did They Do That?)* (Rockport, MA: Rockport, 2003).

Maeda, John. *Creative Code: Aesthetics and Computation* (London/New York: Thames & Hudson, 2004).

Moggridge, Bill. *Designing Interactions* (Cambridge, MA: M.I.T. Press, 2007).

Salen, Katie and Eric Zimmerman. *Rules of Play: Game Design Fundamentals* (Cambridge, MA: M.I.T. Press, 2003).

Solana, Gemma and Antonio Boneu. *The Art of the Title Sequence: Film Graphics in Motion* (London: Collins, 2007).

Wands, Bruce. *Art of the Digital Age* (London/New York: Thames & Hudson, 2007).

Woolman, Matt. *Motion Design: Moving Graphics for Television, Music Video, Cinema, and Digital Interfaces* (London: RotoVision, 2004).

INDEX

ACKNOWLEDGEMENTS

We respectfully and gratefully bow to the designers, past and present, represented in this book. They are exemplars in their field and their collective and individual work is the model on which great graphic design is built.

Sincere gratitude goes to our editor Sophie Drysdale who invited us to do this book and spearheaded it through its conceptual stages. Thanks also to Jo Lightfoot and Felicity Maunder for editorial guidance in the final stages; to Peter Kent for his picture research; and to Here Design and Alex Coco for the design concept and layout. To Christopher Burke, thanks for the Gerd Arntz assistance.

We value the support of various colleagues: Lita Talarico at the School of Visual Arts MFA Design program 'Designer as Author + Entrepreneur', and Joe Newton and Betsy Mei Chun Lin at Anderson Newton Design.

And, as always, a huge thank you to our families: Louise Fili, Nick Heller, Gerry Anderson Arango and Mike Anderson. Thanks for humouring us along the way.

PICTURE CREDITS

11 Staatliche Museen zu Berlin. Photo: Jörg P. Anders © 2015. Photo Scala, Florence/bpk, Bildagentur für Kunst, Kultur und Geschichte, Berlin/© The Josef and Anni Albers Foundation/VG Bild-Kunst, Bonn and DACS, London 2015. **12** Photograph courtesy of Museum für Gestaltung, Zurich, poster collection. **15** David Drummond. **16** Photograph courtesy of Museum für Gestaltung, Zurich, poster collection. **19** Image courtesy Pentagram. **20** Photograph courtesy of Museum für Gestaltung, Zurich, poster collection. **23** Image courtesy the Xanti Schawinsky Estate. **24** Heritage Image Partnership Ltd/ Alamy Stock Photo/© DACS 2015. **26** Digital image, The Museum of Modern Art, New York/Scala, Florence. **28** Image © Stankowski-Stiftung GmbH. **31** Courtesy Brody Associates. © The Coca-Cola Company. **35** Images courtesy Jessica Hische. Client: Penguin Books; Art Direction: Paul Buckley; Associate Publisher & Editorial Director: Elda Rotor. **36** Louise Fili. **39** Private collection. **40** Image courtesy Jonathan Barnbrook. **43** Image courtesy Sawdust. **44** From *Ladislav Sutnar: Visual Design in Action* (1961). Reproduced with permission of the Ladislav Sutnar family. **47** Image courtesy Pentagram. **48** The Herb Lubalin Study Center of Design and Typography/The Cooper Union. **51** By kind permission of the estate of Shigeo Fukuda. **53** Courtesy of the Alan Fletcher Archive. **54** Design: David Gray; photo: Junko Kimura; cover courtesy: Here! Media. **59** Designed by Fons Hickmann, Berlin. **60** Photograph courtesy of Museum für Gestaltung, Zurich, poster collection. **63** Rochester Institute of Technology, Library. **64** Design: Rex Bonomelli. **67** The Paul Rand Revocable Trust. **68** Courtesy Sagmeister & Walsh. **71** © DACS 2015. **72** Estate of Saul Bass. All Rights Reserved. **74** Image courtesy Control Group. **79** From *ZLOM* by Konstantin Biebl (1928), designed by Karel Teige. **81** Courtesy Peter Bankov. **83** Seymour Chwast/Pushpin Group, Inc. **84** Courtesy Marian Bantjes. **87** Private collection, London. **88** (top) Image courtesy Shepard Fairey; (bottom) Image courtesy John Van Hamersveld/ Coolhous Studio. **91** Courtesy Copper Greene. **92** The Estate of Tibor Kalman. **95** Design by Art Chantry. **99** Gift of Clarissa Alcock Bronfman. Acc. No.: 998.2010. © 2015. Digital image, The Museum of Modern Art, New York/Scala, Florence. **100** Otto and Marie Neurath Isotype Collection, University of Reading/© DACS 2015. **103** © HfG-Archiv, Ulmer Museum, Ulm & by permission of Florian Aicher. **104** © Estate of Abram Games. **107** Designed by Steff Geissbuhler. **108** Art direction and design: Paul Sahre; design: Tamara Shopsin. **111** Massin. **112** *The Gettin Place* by Susan Straight, published by Hyperion, 1995. Designer: Michael Schwab; Illustrator: Michael Schwab; Art Director: Victor Weaver; illustration/design © Michael Schwab Studio. **115** The Heartfield Community of Heirs/VG Bild-Kunst, Bonn and DACS London 2015. **116** Courtesy Christoph Niemann. Work commissioned by *Nozone* magazine, editor Nicholas Blechman.